Raccoon John Smith
Frontiersman and Reformer

Everett Donaldson

Wind Publications
Lexington, KY 1993

Raccoon John Smith—Frontiersman and Reformer.
Copyright © 1993 by Everett Donaldson. All rights reserved. Printed in the United States of America. No part of this book may be reproduced in any manner whatsoever without written permission except in the case of brief quotations embodied in critical articles and reviews. For information address Wind Publications, PO Box 24548, Lexington, KY 40524.

Cover illustration by Josie Tipton Sheldon.

Library of Congress Catalog Card Number 93-72516

ISBN 0-9636545-1-9 (pbk)

Second edition

First published in hardcover edition by North Ridge Publishing, Mt. Sterling, Kentucky. Library of Congress Catalog Card Number 91-90612, ISBN 0-9631340-0-0

DEDICATION

To Temple Cope Donaldson, my beloved wife, for her unwavering assistance, devotion, and loyalty during the research and writing of this volume.

Raccoon John Smith 1784-1868

CONTENTS

Acknowledgments   1
Foreword   3
Introduction   5

1. THE OLD DOMINION OF
   GEORGE SMITH (1732-1781)   9
   A Threat to the Established Order
   The Coldness of Calvinism
   The First Great Awakening
   Off to War

2. UPSETTING THE OLD ORDER (1781-1784)   16
   The Persistent Presbyterians
   The Battling Baptists
   Farewell to the Old Dominion

3. TO THE CANAAN OF THE WEST (1765-1795)   23
   Daniel Boone Opens the Way
   A Hazardous Journey
   The Traveling Churches

4. STOCKTON'S VALLEY AND
   THE FORMATIVE YEARS (1796-1804)   34
   The Crab Orchard Fiddler
   Another Dangerous Assignment
   A Calvinist Preacher and a Concerned Mother
   Among the Elect of God
   Peace in the Valley—and Sadness
   The Death of a Patriarch

5. ALONG THE LITTLE SOUTH FORK (1806-1814)   47
   A Land Purchase in Horse Hollow
   Knowledge Bought in the Market
   Home in Horse Hollow
   Ordained to Preach

Contents

6. **THE DARKEST HOUR (1814-1815)** — 59
   Unforgettable Jeremiah Vardeman
   A Vision Beyond Horse Hollow
   A Climate Ripe for Speculation
   A Tragic Venture
   Grief upon Grief

7. **A NEW BEGINNING (1815-1817)** — 69
   The Journey Back
   Return to Crab Orchard
   A Memorable Sermon
   Back Along the Little South Fork
   A New Wife and a New Location

8. **JOHN SMITH'S DIFFICULT FIELD OF LABOR (1801-1818)** — 76
   The North District Association of United Baptists
   The "Destitute" Churches of Montgomery County

9. **A VEXATIOUS INTRODUCTION (1817-1822)** — 81
   Grassy Lick Potpourri
   Contentious Lulbegrud
   Separatist Spencer Creek
   Controversial Mount Sterling
   Economic Hardships
   A Hasty Orientation
   A Frustrated Sermon

10. **THE MERGING OF A MAN AND A MOVEMENT (1798-1822)** — 92
    The Second Great Awakening
    Barton Warren Stone and the Great Revival
    A Recalcitrant Barton Stone
    Rice Haggard and "Christians Simply"
    Alexander Campbell—Late Comer
    Independent Movements

Contents

11. THE DECISIVE YEARS (1822-1826)   100
    A Busy Biennium
    The Country Preacher meets the Bethany Scholar—1824
    The Conversion of Jacob and Matilda Jane Coons—1825
    A Changing Climate
    An Unmistakable Stand—1826

12. GUILTY AS CHARGED (1827-1828)   111
    Lulbegrud Reacts
    Unanticipated Vindication

13. FAREWELL FROM THE BAPTISTS (1829-1831)   116
    James French and Lulbegrud Counterattack
    James Mason and "The Present State of Affairs"
    Historic Concourse at Spencer
    Excluded at Elkhorn
    Reform—A Baptist Nemesis
    Every Man "To His Proper Stand"

14. JEREMIAH VARDEMAN—ENIGMATIC FRIEND
    OF JOHN SMITH (1810-1829)   126
    The Beginning of the End
    A Vacillating Vardeman
    In the Reformer Camp
    Viewing Vardeman from Another Vantage Point
    Exit Vardeman
    Enter Thomas Hansford

15. THE ROAD TO HILL STREET (1823-1832)   138
    A Decade in Retrospect
    Scholarly John T. Johnson
    Smith, Johnson, and the Elkhorn Association
    A Delicate Matter - Enlisting Smith in the Cause of Union

16. HILL STREET PRELIMINARIES (1821-1832)   145
    Peter Hon—Quiet Catalyst?
    Toward Restoration
    Crossing the Demarcation Line
    The Gentle German and the Bold Country Preacher

Contents

17. FORMAL UNION AND ITS WAKE (1832-1834)   154
    "Called on the Carpet"
    Smith and Rogers "to Ride"
    Success in the Counties of Montgomery and Bath
    A Visit Back Home

18. THE END OF AN ERA (1835)   162
    Relief for Nancy
    Farewell to an Old Adversary
    "Indefatigable" John Smith of Montgomery

19. AN OVERVIEW (1836-1868)   168
    Post Meridian of Life
    The "Raccoon" Cognomen
    "A Thousand Pleasing Memories"

    Notes   173
    Bibliography   189
    Index   195

    About the author, Everett Donaldson   199

ACKNOWLEDGMENTS

A debt of gratitude is owed to many capable people whose contributions have made this work possible. Hazel Mason Boyd, co-author of *A History of Mt. Sterling, Kentucky—1792-1918*, was most generous in permitting free access to her extensive files. At intervals, Judge Caswell Lane was helpful in ascertaining the accuracy of particular events.

Roy Horseman, a lifelong friend and fellow elder in the Queen Street Church of Christ in Mt. Sterling, and Dr. R. L. Roberts of Abilene, Texas, made contributions in the research on Peter Hon. Kevin Jenkins, current minister of the Queen Street congregation, Karen Willoughby Rose, instructor in computer education, and Donna Frazier McGuire, secretary to the superintendent of Montgomery County Schools, assisted in the selection of appropriate word processing programs.

Others in the local school system who deserve credit for their helpful suggestions during the preparation of the manuscript are Sue Stull, history instructor, Delores Rawlings Sapp, Instructional Supervisor, Betty Donaldson Collins, English instructor, and Elizabeth Petitt, Coordinator of Gifted Education. Josie Tipton Sheldon, art instructor, presented several sketches in arriving at the author's perception of John Smith and the frontier spirit as portrayed on the cover of the book.

Dr. Richard Hughes, Superintendent of Montgomery County Schools, Mt. Sterling, Kentucky, a former student of the author, carefully examined the manuscript and made beneficial observations. Josephine Howell Tipton, a descendant of the John Coons family, generously shared valuable information which pertained to her pioneer ancestors.

Beyond Montgomery County, Garnett Walker, a respected historian of Wayne County, Kentucky, suggested sources which pertain to Horse Hollow and the Little South Fork region. Archivists

Dorothy Johnson and Reneé Prewitt of Huntsville, Alabama, were most accommodating in locating Hickory Flats and the Miller Cemetery. Sara Bullock of Bluff City, Tennessee, provided significant information relating to the Holston River country where John Smith was born.

My brother-in-law, George Rogers, a diligent student of Barton Warren Stone and events pertaining to Cane Ridge, was most helpful in providing information on pertinent matters related to the Restoration Movement in the Bourbon and Nicholas County areas. Franklin Wade, of Winchester, Kentucky, by his sustained interest, served as a source of encouragement throughout the endeavor.

Remaining are two individuals whose contributions have been absolutely invaluable. A debt of gratitude is due Dr. Adron Doran, President Emeritus of Morehead State University, co-author of The *Christian Scholar* and a renowned student of the Restoration Movement in Kentucky, for serving as a meticulous appraiser of the historical accuracy of the manuscript.

Finally, and most significantly, without the consistent support of Temple Cope Donaldson, my devoted wife, bringing this work to a completion would have been impossible. A perceptive and discriminating proof reader, she was invaluable in assisting with the organization of relevant materials. Serving as chauffeur much of the time, she was a constant companion as we traveled hundreds of miles during the research phase of this work.

Much satisfaction was derived from plying through numerous libraries, courthouses, and old cemeteries in pursuit of information which would assist me in identifying with Raccoon John Smith, frontiersman and reformer, as he experienced triumphs, endured struggles, and suffered tragedies.

— Everett Donaldson

FOREWORD

The author has written one of the most complete biographies that I have ever read of one of the pioneers of the Restoration Movement. It is most difficult for a historian to place in proper perspective individuals, events and places in writing such a factual and dramatic story as *Raccoon John Smith—Frontiersman and Reformer*. However, Everett Donaldson has compiled an excellent piece of work in presenting "Raccoon" John Smith in his true light. This is the first effort of modern day historians to detail specific events, present in perfect order the happenings and to place individuals in their proper relationships as Donaldson has done in handling the life of John Smith.

This publication is the first of a number planned by Everett in his aspirations to bring Smith and Montgomery County, Kentucky, into clearer focus and give them their rightful places in the Restoration Movement. This work reflects the competency of Donaldson as a researcher and scholarly writer.

I have known the author and members of his family since he was a teenager. He was with his parents at the Old Cane Ridge meetinghouse in Bourbon County in 1945 when I first spoke there to an assembly of members of Churches of Christ from Central Kentucky. I have often mentioned that Everett's parents were the latter day examples of John and Nancy Smith.

Everett Donaldson is deeply rooted in the "faith which was once delivered unto the saints" and is well acquainted with the principles and purposes of the Restoration Movement. Donaldson has spent his adult life as a public school teacher and administrator, and as a gospel preacher and elder of the church. His contributions to the Lord's church have been without number and his leadership in public education in Kentucky has influenced the structure of middle school organization in the Commonwealth.

I am highly honored to have the privilege of presenting this volume as a work of the heart and hand of my beloved friend and brother in Christ—Everett Donaldson. The memories regarding the great Reformer and Restorer, John Smith, will live long and intimately in the minds of those who read this choice publication.

— Adron Doran

INTRODUCTION

The original design of the research pertaining to John Smith was the publication of one book. When the collection of materials was organized and the writing had seriously begun, however, it became evident that the scope was beyond the contents of one volume. Therefore, *Raccoon John Smith—Frontiersman and Reformer* will be followed by *Raccoon John Smith—Restoration Preacher* and *The Montgomery County Legacy of Raccoon John Smith*. Each book will be organized in such a way that it will not be dependent upon either of the other publications.

Attention has been given to accommodating the researcher as well as the casual and selective reader. For their convenience and respective purposes an index has been supplied, time parameters have been included with chapter titles, and detailed subtitles have been placed within the Table of Contents.

My late father and mother are primarily due credit for my interest in John Smith. In early 1937 Clyde and Martha Donaldson, who were then twenty-eight and twenty-four years of age respectively, moved with their four small children into the Upper Spencer community of eastern Montgomery County, Kentucky. They began attending the Upper Spencer Christian Church, meeting in a building constructed ninety years previously. As a child of only six summers, it was impossible for me to realize that our family had located in an area exceptionally rich in both secular and religious history.

Soon after becoming active in the Upper Spencer Church, my father, with the assistance of Taylor Lowry of Winchester, Kentucky, took the lead in changing the congregation from a Christian Church to a Church of Christ. That particular transition returned the congregation to its status of a century earlier. In the 1820's Raccoon John Smith, preaching a return to the ancient order, had been responsible for the transition of Spencer Creek Baptist Church to "The Church of Jesus Christ at Spencer Creek," leading it from the Baptist fold into the Restoration Movement. Following John Smith's

Introduction

association with the Spencer Church, however, a gradual decline in membership occurred and many failed to continue sharing his perception of the first century pattern.

During the 1940's the name of Raccoon John Smith was often mentioned by students of the Restoration Movement who came to Upper Spencer, formerly Spencer Creek. Adron Doran and A. H. Kennamer were two who, in terms of a sustained interest, distinguished themselves in restoration history within Montgomery County. An indelible impression was made upon me as I gradually came to realize that we were worshipping in the same building in which the restoration plea had been so effectively proclaimed by the renowned pioneer preacher. Within that context there developed a lasting appreciation for that distinctive plea, and for John Smith, who sacrificed beyond measure to perpetuate it.

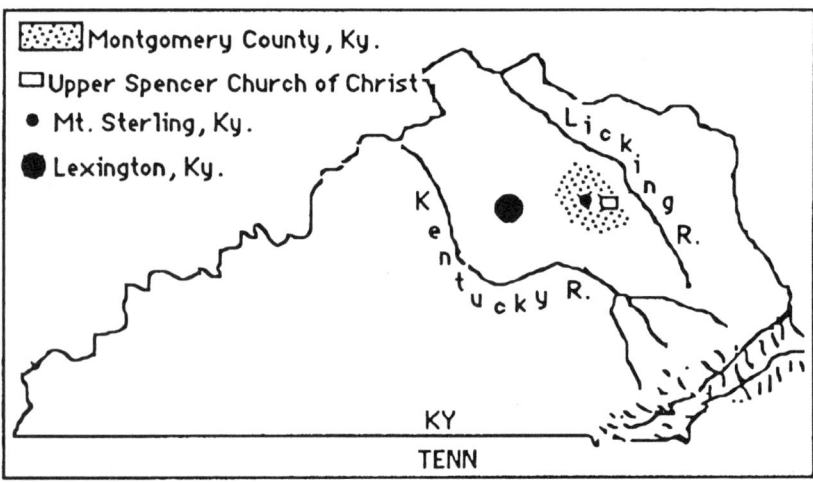

Prior to his death in 1968, one century after the death of the inimitable Raccoon John Smith, my father presented me a folder he had received from an elderly retired superintendent of Montgomery County Schools. It contained a brief historical sketch of the Upper Spencer Church and of the early efforts of John Smith in the community. That presentation constituted the first entry into my files of Smith and the Restoration Movement in Montgomery County. Since that time, hundreds of miles have been traveled and many hours consumed in pursuit of original sources regarding the subject at hand.

Because Smith had assimilated, in great measure, the attributes of his parents, this account begins with George and Rebecca Smith in

Introduction

the back-country of Virginia. Their sturdy characters provided the first ingredients in the development of the rugged individualism of their illustrious son. His determination and willingness to sacrifice, in the interest of what he believed to be right, contributed to his becoming one of the best known preachers on the Kentucky frontier.

Various forces peculiar to the frontier regions of the new Republic contributed to the development of John Smith, who was born only eight years after the signing of the Declaration of Independence. To assist in an appreciation of his pioneer orientation, the political, social, and religious currents of the post revolutionary period which attended the Smith family's move westward are examined.

A frontiersman in the fullest import of the term, Smith lived within the context of a captivating era in the unfolding of young America. Perhaps more than any other preacher of the Restoration Movement, he was the most precise personification of the frontier spirit. Indeed, he was a prodigy of the frontier.

In 1823 Smith was introduced to the *Christian Baptist*, a journal which Alexander Campbell began to publish during the same year. That introduction led Smith to begin considering himself a "Reformer" within the Baptist Church. For a decade he struggled in the interest of reformation among the Baptists. In consideration of the context in which he lived and the design of his early preaching, *Raccoon John Smith—Frontiersman and Reformer* is deemed to be an appropriate title for this particular period of his life.

UPPER SPENCER CHURCH OF CHRIST

In 1845 John Smith served as "Moderator" for a meeting during which a committee was chosen for the purpose of deciding whether the Spencer Creek meetinghouse, built in 1812, should be replaced or repaired. The committee recommended the erection of a new building on the same site. Smith last preached at Spencer in 1865, at the age of eighty-one years. The building continues to be in use.

CHAPTER 1

THE OLD DOMINION OF GEORGE SMITH
(1732-1781)

George Schmidt was born in Germany either during or near the year of 1732. His parents soon departed their native land and migrated to the British colony of Virginia, landing on the American shore in 1735. Inasmuch as Virginia had been the destination of fortune seekers and religious refugees for more than a century prior to the arrival of the Schmidts, the fertile tidewater lands had already been claimed. Therefore, they trudged for more than two hundred miles westward to the headwaters of the James River and settled within the area which became Botetourt County, Virginia.[1]

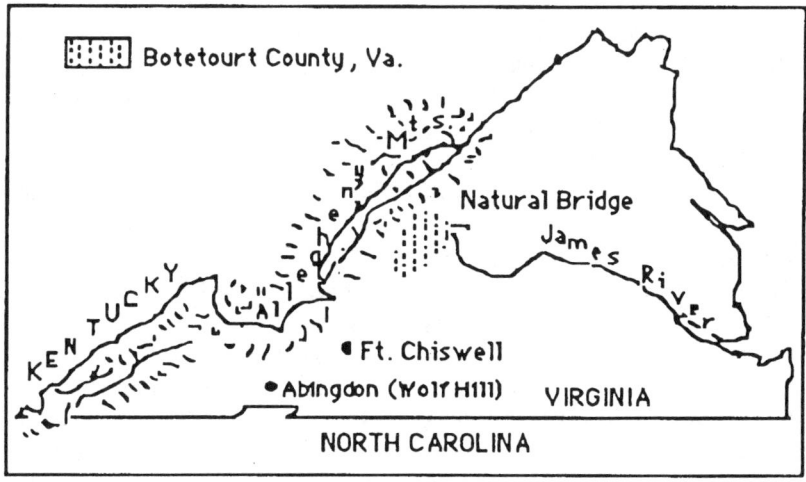

The Schmidts, however, never fully realized the aspirations which they had cherished for themselves and for their young son. Both parents died at an early age, leaving George a lonely orphan, separated by an ocean from the land of his forebears. Fortunately, a compassionate and enterprising neighbor took the lad into his family and he was "faithfully brought up to usefulness and virtue."[2]

A THREAT TO THE ESTABLISHED ORDER

Virginia, the first of the thirteen colonies and the adopted home of young George Schmidt, was the only colony in which provision was made to enforce conformity to the Church of England. This was not especially difficult for the first one hundred years for civil and religious authorities because the Anglicans commanded a clear majority of the religious population. King James I, the same monarch responsible for the "King James Version" of the Bible, in the charter of Virginia explicitly instructed:

> 'The true word and service of God' was to be preached, planted, and 'used' in the new colony 'according to the doctrine, rights [rites?], and religion now professed and established within our realm of England.[3]

Chaplains were appointed and laws were passed with the intention of prohibiting religious dissent. The pattern of religious uniformity, however, began to be shaken by an influx of immigrants of various religious backgrounds. Indeed, the Schmidt family was a part of this immigration which was destined to determine the direction of the subsequent American experience in religious and political liberty.

In addition to Germans who came into the backwoods of Virginia, there were Scots from northern Ireland, those who claimed to be pure Irish, and others who moved south from New England. Within this variety of ethnic backgrounds the Scotch-Irish represented potential Presbyterian strength, while a latent Baptist force resided among the Germans and transplanted New Englanders. It was only a matter of time until upcountry dissenting groups became a serious threat to the established church and the ruling aristocracy of the tidewater region.[4]

In due time, George "Smith," the Anglicized form of Schmidt, married Rebecca Bowen, an Irish maiden. Rebecca's industry and meticulous attention to details complemented the characteristics of her German bred husband. Quiet and peace-loving people, they were driven by the singular desire for economic independence and by a determination to rear their family free of religious and political infringements. These aspirations held special significance for George and Rebecca Smith, considering that their ancestors had braved the perils of the broad Atlantic and the uncertainties of a strange land in pursuit of these elusive freedoms.

THE COLDNESS OF CALVINISM

During their residence in Virginia, the Smiths became associated with the Calvinistic Baptists.[5] This identification guaranteed that they would lead less than tranquil lives in a colony where the Mother Country had imposed an established religion.

The Smiths subscribed to the Calvinistic doctrine of predestination which asserted that an individual was either among the elect group, chosen aforetime by God to be saved eternally, or already at the time of birth among the non-elect group and assigned to an eternal hell. There was nothing the individual could do, regardless of the nature of his life, to alter this decree. Personal experiences, which the Smiths claimed to have had, led them to conclude that they were among the elect of God.

Beginning in the sixteenth century with John Calvin of Geneva, Switzerland, Calvinism, in its purest form, envisioned the state as existing to make laws in accordance with the puritanical ideas of its "pastors." Those pastors were expected to organize schools and to guarantee that a particular ecclesiastical regimen was strictly enforced. The rigorous Calvinistic doctrine made its way to colonial America primarily through the Puritans and Presbyterians who came from England and Scotland. However, to a lesser or greater degree, practically every religious group which landed on the shores of the new land had imbibed some provisions of Calvinism.[6] By its very nature, the doctrine tended to perpetuate a moral pessimism often expressed in hopelessness and religious indifference.

Attributed to Calvinism was a dichotomy in which "the saints might be sinners and the sinners might be saints, if the first would yield to temptation, or the last to urgent entreaty."[7] Despite this paradox, by the time of their marriage in 1766, when George was thirty-three years of age and Rebecca was twenty-four,[8] they had developed into a pious, devout couple, holding firmly to the basic tenets of the Philadelphia Confession of Faith, the creed of the "Old Light" or Regular Baptists. So while not acknowledging the free moral agency of the individual, the Smiths still read the Bible faithfully in their home, and their children were exhorted to:

Seek after God, if, haply, they might find him; yet to esteem themselves dead, and to bide the good time when, unless predestined to eternal wrath, the mysterious Spirit would give them life, and open their eyes to the beauties of a Saviour.[9]

It is most likely that George and Rebecca Smith were well aware of and deeply concerned about the religious revivals which began punctuating the regimented climate of backwoods Virginia during their residence there. A type of preaching was introduced which declared that conversion was essential and that a godly life held great promise. Even though the religious awakening during the middle decades of the eighteenth century appeared to do little to resolve the contradictions posed by Calvinism, at least the new movement placed a renewed emphasis upon individual choice and righteous living.

THE FIRST GREAT AWAKENING

History records two great spiritual awakenings in early America. These religious revivals, one preceding the War for American Independence and the other following the conflict, had a significant effect upon the development of the young nation, the amelioration of a harsh frontier, and the eventual design to restore first century Christianity.

The first awakening, beginning in New England during the third decade of the eighteenth century, was initiated by a reaction to the rigid formalism and lack of spiritual vitality within existing religious institutions. Credited with providing the initial impetus for the First Great Awakening was Solomon Stoddard, the popular minister who preached in Northampton, Massachusetts for sixty years (1669-1729). During a time when Puritanism had become stale and ritualistic, Stoddard began declaring to his congregation and fellow ministers: "We are not sent into the pulpit to shew our wit and eloquence, but to set the consciences of men on fire."[10] He struck with force at the cold formalism and religious indifference of his day.

A contemporary of Stoddard was Theodore Jacob Frelinghuysen, a gifted minister who came from Holland to preach to New Jersey Dutch immigrants. Frelinghuysen shared Stoddard's notion that personal conversion, accompanied by a life of obedient faith and love, were absolute essentials in following Christ. He vigorously attacked what he considered to be a repulsive state of indifference and ungodliness. He asserted that:

Great laxity of manners prevailed throughout his charge...while horse-racing, gambling, dissipation, and rudeness of various kinds were common, the [church] was attended at convenience, and religion consisted of the mere formal pursuit of the routine of duty.

Two famous evangelists followed Stoddard and Frelinghuysen, fanning the fires which had been kindled by them. George Whitefield and Jonathan Edwards, the latter a grandson of Stoddard, became recognized as spiritual giants in colonial America. At the height of his preaching career Edwards stirred New England with sermons such as his famous "Sinners in the Hands of an Angry God," preached in Enfield, Connecticut in 1741. Whitefield, known as the "Episcopal Lightning Rod," made several voyages from England to preach in the American colonies.

William Tennent, a Presbyterian inspired by the efforts of Frelinghuysen, began training preachers in the "Log College" located on his farm northwest of Philadelphia. Graduates of his "New Light" school, so designated by its critics, did much to change the religious landscape of the middle colonies. Regarded as the "School of the Prophets" by its friends, this institution trained preachers who continued to perpetuate the religious fervor previously generated by Stoddard, Frelinghuysen, Edwards, and Whitefield.[11]

Samuel Davies, one of the "Log College" graduates and later president of Princeton University, pushed the movement farther south. Among Baptists prominent in spreading the revival fires into Virginia and North Carolina were Shubel Sterns and his brother-in-law, Daniel Marshall, both products of New England revivalism.[12]

William Screven, considered to be the father of South Carolina and Southern Baptists, is credited with planting the Baptist Church not only in South Carolina, but in all of the southern colonies.[13] He fell victim very early to religious persecution in New England for opposing infant baptism. Following a fine and jail sentence, further abuse was avoided by his promising to leave Maine. After receiving land in South Carolina by purchase and by grant, Screven and other emigrants from Maine formed the nucleus of a Baptist Church at Summerton. The church moved into Charleston either during or near the year 1693.[14]

Even though the revivals in colonial America are considered by many to have had positive effects, the movement began losing its dynamism after a quarter of a century. Anything which resembled the fires ignited by these early eighteenth century preachers was reserved for post revolutionary turn-of-the-century frontier America, an era designated by historians as The Second Great Awakening.

OFF TO WAR

The prohibition of religious liberty by the established church of Virginia was compounded by England's political and economic oppression of the colonies. Resistance to such oppression resulted in the British attack of the Minute Men at Lexington and Concord, thus precipitating the War for American Independence. This turn of events proved to be very disruptive to the domestic aspirations of George and Rebecca Smith.

Smith's readiness to shoulder his gun and leave the farm and his family while he joined the revolution against the Mother Country was indicative of his insatiable aspiration for religious liberty. This active involvement in the conflict came with much sacrifice, inasmuch as he was forty-three years old and a father of five children at the time the hostilities began.[15]

Like other colonial rebels Smith had in mind both liberation from the tyranny of the "Tories," as British sympathizers in the colonies were known, and the severance of attachments with autocratic King George III. The disdain of the colonists was perhaps best expressed by Thomas Payne, who dubbed the British monarch a "Royal Brute."[16]

The experiences which came to the Smiths both before and during the war provided them a fiercely independent orientation which enabled them to adapt not only to the rigorous life of backwoods Virginia, but to the subsequent frontiers of East Tennessee, and eventually to the harsh "Dark and Bloody Ground" of far off Kentucky.

From a bridge which spans the James River in Botetourt County, Virginia, the author surveys the rugged landscape of the area where George and Rebecca Bowen Smith lived before their migration to the State of Franklin.

CHAPTER 2

UPSETTING THE OLD ORDER
(1781-1784)

When the struggle with England had ended, George Smith returned to his family and resumed his farming. His children now numbered eight, two daughters and a son having been born during the war years.[1] Unfortunately, any notion of quietly settling permanently on his Botetourt County homestead and rearing his family free of interference was soon to be revised.

It was apparent that religious liberty, as well as political freedom, was a significant issue for back-country Virginians when the colonies challenged the mighty British crown. However, soon after the abrupt ending of hostilities in the fall of 1781, many Virginia dissenters such as Smith experienced deep disappointment when it became apparent that complete religious freedom was not an immediate companion of political independence from the Mother Country. Even though the Tories returned to England, or adopted a low profile among the masses, it was evident that the religious pressures and prejudices of the prewar era still prevailed. Consequently, other battles remained to be fought.

Following the War for Independence, the Episcopal Church continued to be recognized as the official religion in Virginia for more than a decade. Citizens of that Commonwealth, regardless of their church affiliation, were taxed to support the Episcopalian clergy, and any activity considered to be a serious threat to the dominance of the state church was not ignored.[2] Such a condition of religious tyranny imposed upon a dissenting people, who had recently gained their political independence from the British crown, could not long endure. In portraying their disdain for the established religion, the persecuted dissenters likened themselves to the Hebrew children of the Scriptures who refused to bow down to the golden image of the Babylonian Nebuchadnezzar of their age.[3]

Upsetting the Old Order

The Presbyterians and Baptists led the charge in this second revolt against an established religion and its civil accomplice. These two denominations shared much in common, inasmuch as the Philadelphia Confession of Faith of the American Baptists was no more than a slightly amended version of the Westminster Confession of Faith of the Presbyterians.[4] Sharing the basic tenets of Calvinism, they differed only on the mode and design of baptism and in organizational structure. In their aspirations for freedom their objectives were the same.

The Methodists soon took advantage of concessions gained by the Presbyterians and Baptists, and with extraordinary zeal, most evident in their circuit riders, spread Methodism across the frontier. These three groups are significant to the purpose of this account since it was from their ranks that the nineteenth century Restoration Movement was spawned. Many of their talented preachers rebelled against their sectarian creeds.

THE PERSISTENT PRESBYTERIANS

Abhorrence of a monarch who interfered with individual liberties in matters of religion was nothing new among Presbyterians who came to America. King James I of England, when speaking of a rebellious Scotch Presbytery, is quoted as having said: "Presbytery agreeth as well with monarchy as God and the devil."[5] Therefore, Presbyterian resistance to the established order in Virginia was simply an extension of what had been transpiring back in the old country.

Sources agree that the Scotch-Irish Presbyterians generally detested Catholics, the enemies of their forefathers, and despised the Episcopalians, Catholicism's successors of oppression in the new land. Of that group which first came to Virginia, it is recorded:

> That the Irish Presbyterians were a bold and hardy race is proved by their at once pushing past the settled regions and plunging into the wilderness as the leaders of the white advance....The creed of the backwoodsmen who had a creed at all was Presbyterian, for the Episcopacy of the tidewater lands obtained no foothold in the mountains, and the Methodists and Baptists had but just begun to appear in the west before the Revolution broke out.[6]

The backwoods Presbyterians were charged by an agent of the royal crown as being the primary culprits in the mischief wrought against the Mother Country. "When this war is over," the charge continued, "it will become apparent that Presbyterianism is really at the bottom of the whole conspiracy."[7] One source summarized the scenario by observing:

> The theology of Calvin, the founder of the republic of Geneva, combined with the sturdy independence of the Scotch-Irish settlers of the American colonies, gave birth to our republic. The first voice raised in America to destroy all connection with Great Britain came from the Scotch-Irish Presbyterians.[8]

With the advantage of numbers, wealth, and learned and able leaders, the Presbyterians were equipped to continue the struggle until the objective of complete religious liberty was realized. They also enjoyed a measure of prestige because of their recognized contribution to the success of the revolt against the British. Lovers of liberty such as Thomas Jefferson, Patrick Henry, and James Madison identified with their cause and gradually conditioned the political and religious climate of the Old Dominion for an eventual granting of religious concessions.[9]

THE BATTLING BAPTISTS

Eighteenth century Virginia Baptists primarily came from England, Maryland, and New England. Those coming from England settled in the southeastern part of Virginia while the Maryland Baptists crossed the southern border of that colony and settled in the northwest. Baptists from New England entered the backwoods of Virginia and settled up and down the Shenandoah Valley, crowding the Piedmont Plateau. This last group became most significant in determining the course of religious freedom in the Old Dominion.

When George Whitefield came from Britain to New England for preaching tours, he created what became known as the "New Light Stir."[10] Following his revivals, a dispute arose among Baptists dividing them into "Old Lights," or Regulars, who distrusted revivals and emotionalism, and "New Lights," or Separatists, who were generally given to emotionalism and demanded a reborn membership in their churches.[11] Separatist Baptists, who chose to migrate to Virginia to escape the pressures of the old order in New England, took the lead among Baptist groups in resisting the mandates of the established church and civil authority which supported her.

Presbyterians were rather effective in pursuing their objectives through formal channels within the legal system. The Separatist Baptists, because of their informality, gained much attention outside such channels and brought down upon themselves the wrath of those who felt it their responsibility to protect long standing religious traditions. One historian observed:

> The Baptists drew folks with a vociferous style of preaching that went beyond the word into shouts and drones, thunderous hand clapping, and the ecstatic twisting and jerking of the body itself. The emotional rituals of the new sect, which included fervent handclasps and kisses along with baptism by total immersion, turned congregations into communities, and the great springtime association camp meetings drew several thousand together in a swelling social fellowship.[12]

In addition to strange and emotional meetings, civil authorities of the Old Dominion envisioned the specter of peasant uprisings and religious revolt because the Baptists accepted slaves into their fellowship. In an attempt to stifle the militancy of preachers, whom they considered to be a threat to the church of their fathers, several rather harsh measures were adopted. Many were jailed for disturbing the peace and cases of inhumane treatment are on record.[13]

One such case was that of David Barrow, a Baptist preacher much respected for his training and ability. On one occasion, after being taken from a platform erected under some trees, he was dragged to a muddy pond. His attackers informed him: "As you are fond of dipping, you shall have enough of it."

After plunging Barrow into the water and holding him in a submerged position for an extended time, it is reported that he was asked: "Do you now believe?"

Following the third dunking and the same inquiry, Barrow intimated his disdain for recanting by answering: "I *believe* you are going to drown me."[14]

The persecuted preacher recovered and later migrated to Mt. Sterling, Kentucky, where he served as minister for many years.

Lewis Craig, of historic Spotsylvania County, Virginia, stands out among those who paid heavily for his zeal in preaching during this time of religious oppression. Jailed in Fredericksburg, and indicted by a grand jury "for holding unlawful conventicles and preaching the gospel contrary to law," he continued to preach to large crowds through the grating on his cell windows. During one of Craig's court appearances the prosecuting attorney introduced the accused to the judge and jury by saying, "May it please your worships, these men are great disturbers of the peace; they cannot meet a man on the road, but that they must ram a text of scripture down his throat."[15]

While the Baptists had oppressors among civil authorities, they shared with the Presbyterians two of the greatest champions among those who detested the injustices of religious oppression. James Madison and Patrick Henry were unrelenting in their pursuit to assist religious leaders in attaining their objectives. With the strong support of Baptists, Methodists, and Presbyterians, Madison introduced into the 1789 Congress the First Amendment, which asserted that the United States would have no law establishing religion, a concept then rare in the world.

With the skillful maneuvering of the patient James Madison, the prized amendment acknowledging the inalienable rights of all American citizens was ratified in 1791. During a time when his colleagues were relenting and speaking of religious toleration, the scholarly Madison maintained that, without qualification, the free exercise of religion should be an absolute natural right not subject in any way to the toleration of others.[16] With his pen he established himself as "The Father of the Constitution," while with his tongue the fiery Patrick Henry of "Give me liberty or give me death" fame gave no rest to the established order.

On one occasion during a time of heavy persecution it was reported that Patrick Henry detoured fifty miles from his route to volunteer his services to Baptists jailed in Spotsylvania County. He walked into the courtroom on the day of the trial and heard the reading of the charge against the preachers. Understanding that they were charged with disturbing the peace, he asked to see the indictment.[17]

"Did I hear it distinctly, or was it a mistake of my own?" he inquired. "Did I hear an expression, as of a crime, that these men, whom your worships are about to try for misdemeanor, are charged with—with—what? *Preaching* the Gospel of the Son of God?!"

As only he could do, the clever Henry paused and exploited the period of silence which followed. He held high the paper on which the indictment was written and slowly waved it three times around his head. Then, with face and arms raised toward heaven, he forcefully exclaimed, "Great God!" and again, "Great God!" and, once more, "Preaching the gospel of the Son of God—Great God!" The prosecution, the story concludes, could make no rejoinder, and the sheriff was ordered to release the accused.[18]

FAREWELL TO THE OLD DOMINION

It is not known to what extent George Smith became actively involved in the postwar religious drama which rapidly unfolded around him on the Virginia frontier. Being Regular Baptist, he perhaps looked with suspicion upon the emotional revivals of the Separatists, but he certainly shared their disdain for the established order and its attempts to perpetuate the policies and practices of the old prewar oppressive aristocracy. It is difficult to fathom the frustration of a devoted religious man who had endured the rigors of the War for Independence, as Smith had, only to learn afterwards that proscription, for the sake of opinion, was not at an end.[19]

When it became evident that the legacy of the monarchy of England would continue to prevail in Virginia for an indefinite period of time, the Smiths made a significant decision. Early in 1784, three years following the close of the war, the peace-loving George and Rebecca Smith disposed of their homestead and quietly moved from the headwaters of the James River.

Living near the Old Indian Trace which led to the southwest, George and Rebecca Smith had certainly been aware of the increased numbers to whom the lure of the newly opened West appealed. Subsequently, they chose to join those who were leaving behind the prejudices and hoary sophistication of the Old Dominion. Some were going to the Holston River valley, stopping short of the great mountain barrier to the west, while others chose to brave the hazards of Cumberland Gap and settle in the Virginia county of Kentucky.

The family of five boys and three girls, ranging from Philip, age fifteen, down to two-year-old William,[20] slowly made its way southwestward along the Trace, driving livestock and taking whatever household and personal effects their crude means of conveyance would accommodate. Their destination was the valley of the Holston, located in what eventually became the extreme northeastern portion of the state of Tennessee. Smith was perhaps drawn to this area by his knowledge of a group of Baptists of his persuasion which had recently migrated to that part of the frontier.[21]

Originally, the Smith family settled in territory claimed by North Carolina. The area, however, was isolated from the remainder of the state because it was located on the western edge of the mountain range. Feeling the geographic and political detachment, the settlers organized the State of Franklin, named in honor of Benjamin Franklin, the renowned colonial statesman and inventor. When the proposed new state failed in its attempt to become sovereign, it became a part of Tennessee, which was admitted to statehood in 1796.[22]

Soon after settling in this second location, Rebecca Smith gave birth to John, her ninth child.[23] John Smith, who would become by far the best known of their posterity, inherited his parents' drive for religious liberty and subsequently applied that obsession to emancipation from sectarian creeds, including even the creed of his parents' denomination. In eventually becoming one of the most forceful preachers of the Restoration Movement, he pushed that heritage of liberation far beyond the bounds established by his pious and freedom loving father and mother.

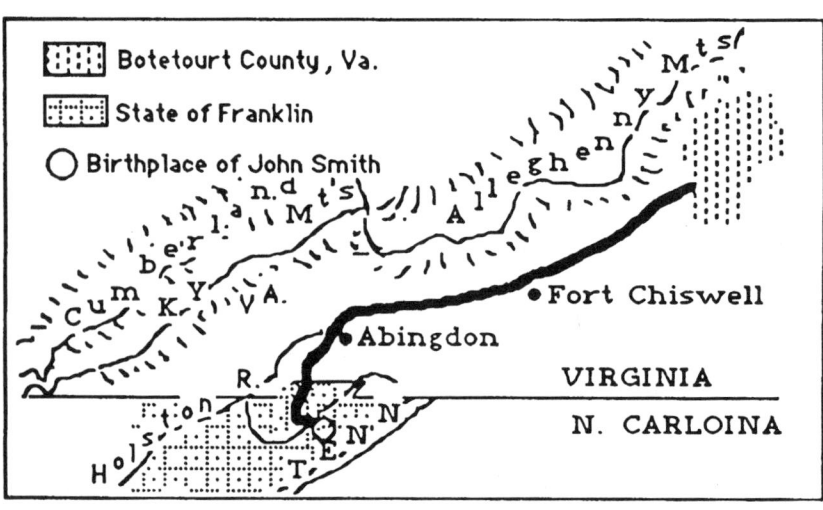

In 1784 George Smith moved his family from Botetourt County, Virginia, to an area along the South Fork of the Holston River, which was located in the newly created State of Franklin.

CHAPTER 3

TOWARD THE CANAAN OF THE WEST
(1765-1795)

John Smith was born on October 15, 1784, in a cabin on the banks of the Holston River. This area eventually became Sullivan County, Tennessee. In this new location, his father and older brothers cleared the land, acre by acre, until the family farm was adequate for their support. The Smiths, believing that idleness was a vice, were determined to demonstrate to their children that hard work was virtuous.

POSSIBLE BIRTH SITE OF JOHN SMITH
It is believed that the cabin in which John Smith was born stood near the east (right) bank of the South Fork of the Holston River.

As soon as John Smith was old enough to do so, he began following his father about the farm and through the forest. By the time he was six or seven years old, he assumed his share of the many chores associated with the rugged farm life of the frontier family. It was here that John received his longest stint in a formal education setting, a total of four months.

After living eleven years in the Holston Valley, George Smith determined that the area would not serve well the long term welfare of his family. Settlers had continued to stream into the area, and acquiring additional land to accommodate a large family had become too expensive. Therefore, deciding to plunge into the wilderness again, he chose to cross through Cumberland Gap in 1795 and follow the Wilderness Road into Kentucky.[1]

To appreciate the struggles, dangers, and uncertain future faced by pioneer families, such as that of George Smith, it is appropriate to briefly examine the hazards of the journey to the West. In doing so, one is perhaps permitted to capture, at least in part, a measure of the frontier spirit so well personified in the Smith family.

DANIEL BOONE OPENS THE WAY

In 1775 Colonel Richard Henderson of the Transylvania Company, envisioning a sovereign land west of the mountains, completed a treaty with the Cherokee Indians at Sycamore Shoals in East Tennessee. The terms of the treaty provided for the purchase of all land between the Cumberland River to the south and the Kentucky River to the north. Henderson immediately began making arrangements for Daniel Boone, who was present when the treaty was negotiated, to open a route into the newly purchased territory.

Boone, who had made two previous excursions into Kentucky, immediately enlisted thirty woodsmen and hacked a trail through the wilderness into the new land. By 1776, the year of the signing of the Declaration of Independence, the Kentucky wilderness had begun yielding to the conquest of the pioneer.[2] However, there were immediate obstacles thwarting the ambitious plans of Henderson and Boone.

In addition to the refusal of the states of Virginia and North Carolina to recognize the legitimacy of Henderson's aspirations, the expected flow of settlers onto the "Dark and Bloody Ground" was stymied when Kentucky became the western front of the War for American Independence. The danger posed by Indian attack became especially severe after the British enlisted those Indians into their

Toward the Canaan of the West

cause. Aided by the arms and military strategy of the British soldiers, the Indians were very effective in launching attacks against outposts on the Kentucky frontier.[3]

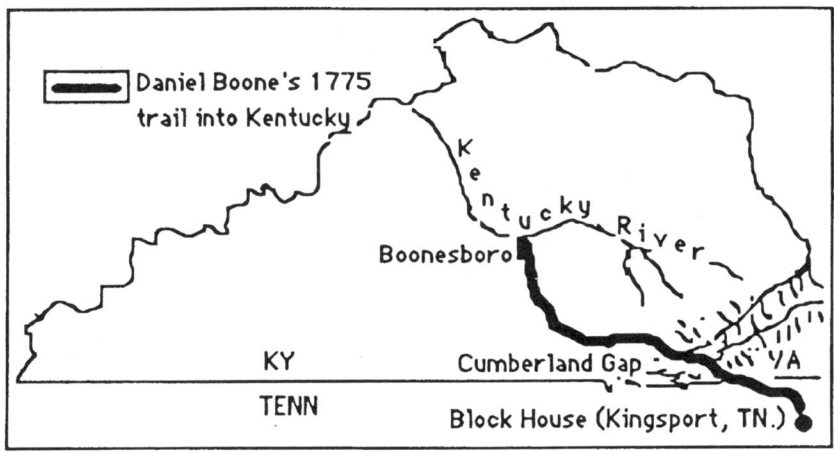

Even though the hostilities of the Revolutionary War did not end until the defeat of Cornwallis at Yorktown, Virginia, in 1781, the grip of the British on the South and West was weakened as early as 1778. This was a consequence of victories by Nathaniel Greene and other patriots in the Carolinas and by General George Rogers Clark in campaigns in the Northwest.[4] The weakening of the British, accompanied by a slight mitigation of the Indian menace, revived within many the determination to realize the fulfillment of dreams inspired by the reports of such explorers as Dr. Thomas Walker, Daniel Boone, and John Finley.

Motives prompting the movement west to the Bluegrass Region were varied. While many came for the promise of land and wealth, others, obsessed with the mystique of the new land beyond the forbidding Appalachian Mountain Range, came simply for adventure. Even though it is not possible to ascertain an accurate percentage, many who migrated to Kentucky were prompted primarily by religious motives. In addition to the promise of land and the reported beauty of a pristine paradise, they definitely would be far removed from the prejudices and abuses which accompanied religious intolerance.

Differing motives of those who first viewed the Kentucky landscape prompted varying reports. John Taylor, one of the first preachers who crossed the mountains, wrote, "It was a gloomy thing at that time of day to come to Kentucky." However, in 1776, William Hickman, credited with preaching the first "Baptist sermon" in the new land, said of his first view:

> When we came to the beauty of the country, I thought of the Queen of Sheba, that came from the uttermost parts of the earth to hear the wisdom of Solomon, and she said the half was not told. So I thought of Kentucky; I thought if I never could get but ten acres of land, I determined to move to it.[5]

Whatever the reactions by those who first viewed it, the allurement of the country beyond the mountains was enhanced for those who desired land, adventure, and religious liberty divested of all infringements.

A HAZARDOUS JOURNEY

Before admitting the white man into Kentucky, Cumberland Gap had been previously traveled only by the buffalo and Indian. In 1750 Dr. Thomas Walker and five companions, exploring in the interest of the Loyal Land Company, entered Kentucky through the most accessible mountain pass and named it in honor of the Duke of Cumberland.[6] Until the discovery of this saddle-like feature the Appalachian Mountain chain appeared as an interminable barrier to the early immigrants.

The wilds and wonders of Cumberland Gap and the Wilderness Road have tapped the literary genius of many writers. In 1893, Frederick Jackson Turner wrote:

> Stand at Cumberland Gap and watch the procession of civilization, marching single file—the buffalo following the trail to the salt springs, the Indian, the fur-trader and hunter, the cattle-raiser, the pioneer farmer—and the frontier has passed by.[7]

Regardless of the romantic verse of the poets and the captivating stories of the novelists, objective historians have recorded that there were genuine hazards and indescribable discomforts for those who swelled the tide of emigration into the land beyond the mountains. James Lane Allen's impressive analogy comparing the challengers of Cumberland Gap to an ant colony provided a vivid and accurate portrayal of the early westward movement. Depicting Kentucky as a big foot whose heel was never ceded by Virginia, Allen wrote:

It was through this heel that Kentucky had to be peopled. The thin, half-starved, weary line of pioneer civilizers had to penetrate it, and climb this obstructing mountain wall, as a line of travelling ants might climb the wall of a castle. In this case only the strongest of the ants—the strongest in body, the strongest in will—succeeded in getting over and establishing their colony in the country far beyond. Luckily there was an enormous depression in the wall, or they might never have scaled it....The feeblest of the ants could not climb the wall; the idlest of them would not. Observe, too, once on the other side, it was as hard to get back as it had been to get over. That is, the Cumberland Mountain kept the little ultramontane society isolated.[8]

Traveling the Wilderness Road continued to be very dangerous for many years, primarily because the Indians perceived the coming of the white man as an intrusion into their legitimate hunting grounds. Of the "Dark and Bloody Grounds" respected Kentucky historian Thomas Clark has written:

Since it was known that this beautiful land was the home of no one, danger threatened those who attempted to claim it. Rival Indian tribes hunted in it, crossed and recrossed it, but seldom, if ever, lingered. It had numerous streams, the delight of every savage heart; it had springs, salt licks, and game in abundance. But always the Indian homes were north of the Ohio or south of the Cumberland.[9]

Since the warpath of the Shawnee shared a section of Boone's Road, and the land of the Cherokee overlapped the southern portion of the western route, there was no way for settlers moving west to avoid the Indians. The danger was compounded by the Chickamauga, who refused to acknowledge the provisions of any treaty with the white man. This recalcitrant tribe continued to prey upon vulnerable pioneers until 1794. In that year tough Indian fighter Colonel William Whitley gathered a force of vindictive frontiersmen and attacked their bases of operation along the Tennessee River.[10]

In 1784 more than one hundred men, women, and children were murdered as they traveled the Wilderness Road from Cumberland Gap to Crab Orchard, Kentucky, a fact indicative of the danger confronted by those who chose the southern route.[11] An example of the type of atrocities recorded as perpetrated by the Indians is given in the following description of a Cherokee attack:

After killing and scalping the white men, confiscating their goods, and drinking their whiskey, the Indians cut up the bodies and proceeded to cook and eat the chunks of the human flesh. Presumably this act was designed to indicate red prowess rather than to satisfy mere hunger.[12]

The family of Peter Cartwright, legendary Methodist circuit rider of more than half a century, came through Cumberland Gap and over the Wilderness Road either during or soon after 1785. The wisdom of traveling with a large contingent is graphically demonstrated in the account of their journey. It was reported that: "They joined a large caravan for protection from the Indians, and their prudence was soon proved when seven families lagged behind and were massacred." [13]

Bishop Francis Asbury, obsessed with the aspiration to establish a Wilderness Road Circuit, made his first visit into Kentucky in 1790. Being well aware of the dangers on the route, he was accompanied by a guard of ten well armed men. Arriving at Masterson's Station, five miles northwest of Lexington, he reported that he "saw the graves of the slain—twenty-four in one camp, who had, a few nights previous, been murdered by the Indians." He decried the "torture of journeying through a dreary wilderness, replete with dangers and infested by savages." [14]

In addition to the Indian threats, criminals escaping justice and roving bands of robbers and thieves preyed upon individuals and small groups which could be overpowered. A fate similar to that which befell the unattended biblical traveler who journeyed from Jerusalem down to Jericho was repeated many times along the dangerous route. Among this sordid group were the infamous Harpes, two of the craftiest and most vicious criminals on the frontier. The very mention of the names of these sons of a North Carolina Tory wreaked terror in the hearts of pioneers for a decade.[15]

Beyond the dangers of traveling the Wilderness Road, the discomforts of such a journey could be endured only by the strong-hearted. Another of Francis Asbury's excursions into Kentucky occurred in 1793, two years before young John Smith traveled the same route with his father and older brother. Of his own discomforts, and those of others which he observed, Asbury wrote:

> A man who is well mounted will scorn to complain of the roads, when he sees men, women, and children, almost naked, paddling barefoot and bare-legged along or laboring up the rocky hills, whilst those who are best off have only a horse for two or three children to ride at once. If these adventurers have little or nothing to eat, it is not an extraordinary circumstance, and not uncommon

> to encamp in the wet woods after night; in the mountains it does not rain, but pours.
>
> I, too, have my sufferings, perhaps peculiar to myself; pain and temptation, the one of the body, the other of the spirit. No room to retire to, that in which you sit common to all, crowded with women and children, the fire occupied by cooking, much and long loved solitude not to be found unless you choose to run out into the rain in the woods....The people it must be confessed are amongst the kindest in the world. But kindness will not make a crowded log cabin, twelve feet by ten, agreeable; without, cold and rain, and within, six adults and as many children, one of which is all motion.
>
> I found amongst my other trials I have taken the itch; and, considering the filthy houses and filthy beds I have met with...it is perhaps strange that I have not caught it twenty times. I do not see that there is any security against it but by sleeping in a brimstone shirt.[16]

Many of the preachers of various religious groups who braved the journey to the harsh frontier beyond the forbidden wall of mountains eventually came to champion the plea to restore the New Testament order of the church. Among them was Samuel Rogers, who journeyed through Cumberland Gap with his family in 1793, the same year as one of Bishop Asbury's uncomfortable treks and approximately two years before the Gap was opened to wagon traffic. Several years later he remembered how the early families moved along the wilderness trails and related:

> A few rude culinary instruments, with bread and meat for the journey, constituted the contents of one end of a large sack, called a wallet, made somewhat after the fashion of saddlebags; while a small bed and bedding, with now and then a little fellow too small to retain his equilibrium on horseback, were ordinarily stowed away in the other, the head of the little one protruding just far enough for breathing purposes. The mother sat enthroned between this moving kitchen and nursery, guiding the horse and administering to the wants of the babies, while the proud father with unerring rifle on his shoulder, and his faithful dog by his side, led the way, dreaming of the contentment in the Canaan of the West.[17]

The majority of the early settlers of Montgomery County, Kentucky, future home of John Smith, were among the thousands who made their way through Cumberland Gap and along the Wilderness Road. At Hazel Patch, located eight miles north of present day London, Kentucky, and thirty-two miles east of Crab Orchard, the main trail veered to the west, while the section known as Boone's Trace continued in a northward direction. Those whose destination was the area which eventually became the county of Montgomery took the trail north to Boonesboro.[18] There they crossed the Kentucky River and, along tomahawk-marked Harper's Trace,[19] struck a northeast course to the foothills of the mountain range which had forced them so far south to circumvent it.

As previously indicated, Indians consistently attacked small groups. Thus the larger the group, the safer the journey. In addition to many detachments of various sizes over a period of years, two large migrations had a direct effect upon Montgomery County and the contiguous areas.

EAST WALL OF APPALACHIAN MOUNTAINS
The forbidding east wall of the Appalachian Mountain chain prevented a direct route into Kentucky by early pioneers. Just southwest of the area shown, Cumberland Gap provided a passageway into the "Cannan of the West."

THE TRAVELING CHURCHES

The most impressive group that ever moved along the Wilderness Road was the Upper Spotsylvania Baptist Church. It is possible that the congregation had grown weary of harassment from the state church and civil authorities and had desired to exchange such prohibitions for the freedom of the Kentucky frontier. If this were the case, then it is conceded that they were inspired to move by the magnetism of Lewis Craig, their respected minister. It is also suggested that Craig had individually decided to go as a missionary to the wild and riotous West, and when he announced his decision, the congregation decided to accompany him.

The large contingent departed Spotsylvania County, Virginia, in September of 1781, the month before General George Washington forced the surrender of Lord Cornwallis and brought an abrupt end to the Revolutionary War. Occurring ten years before the ratification of the First Constitutional Amendment, which gave full religious liberty, this exodus was no small affair. In addition to the church members, their children and Negro slaves, there were emigrants who, for better protection, had attached themselves to the organized expedition. The procession was composed of five or six hundred pioneers, the largest group of Virginians to ever depart for Kentucky at one time. Moving single file, the line stretched three miles along the trail.[20]

Traveling during the late fall and winter months in order to minimize dangers of Indian attacks resulted in extreme hardships for members of this particular group. This journey constituted one of the most impressive accounts of sacrifice contained in the annals of Kentucky history. Their difficulties in part are detailed in the following accounts:

> Most of the men and some of the women were on foot, the others being on horseback, or, in case of illness, on litters. As the journey progressed, and traveling became more difficult, they were forced to abandon, piece by piece, many of their cherished household possessions, and those who had been taught to shun the 'night air' were glad to find shelter for sleep under leafy boughs cut and leaned against a tree.

> But worse was to come. Their store of bread became moldy, freezing weather set in, the sheltering leaves disappeared, and after an attack by the Indians, they were afraid to kindle fires. At

one time the sleet and snow delayed them so that they traveled only thirty miles in three weeks. Throughout all these trials, however, they never lost hope, nor failed to set apart time for worship.[21]

Those who were motivated by an intense desire for total religious freedom, such as members of Lewis Craig's Traveling Church, considered the trek down the Valley of Virginia, through the Gap, and along the Wilderness Road as a journey to "The Western Canaan." They eventually settled on Gilbert's Creek, approximately two and one-half miles southeast of the present town of Lancaster, Kentucky.[22]

The second "Traveling Church," also known as the Bush Colony, was initially formed by Captain Billy Bush. The original group, which consisted of forty families, departed for Kentucky in the fall of 1780, one year earlier than the Lewis Craig contingent. However, Indian dangers resulted in their being delayed along the Holston River (the area which later became Abingdon, Virginia) until the fall of 1783. In September of that year they were organized into a church with Robert Elkin as the "pastor." The group eventually settled north of the Kentucky River in Clark County as Providence Baptist Church. After two centuries the old stone building of the original Providence Church is still standing.[23]

The military commandant for the first "Traveling Church" was Captain William Ellis. Captain Ellis had received a one thousand acre tract of land which extended eastwardly along the north side of Spencer Creek in Montgomery County. The acre upon which the building for Spencer Creek Baptist Church was eventually constructed was carved from the Ellis land grant. Robert Elkin of Providence Church and Moses Bledsoe of Mt. Sterling are credited with organizing the congregation.[24] Therefore, in the legacy of both traveling churches was the Spencer Creek Church, where the transition of Raccoon John Smith from Baptist to Reformer became most evident.

Toward the Canaan of the West

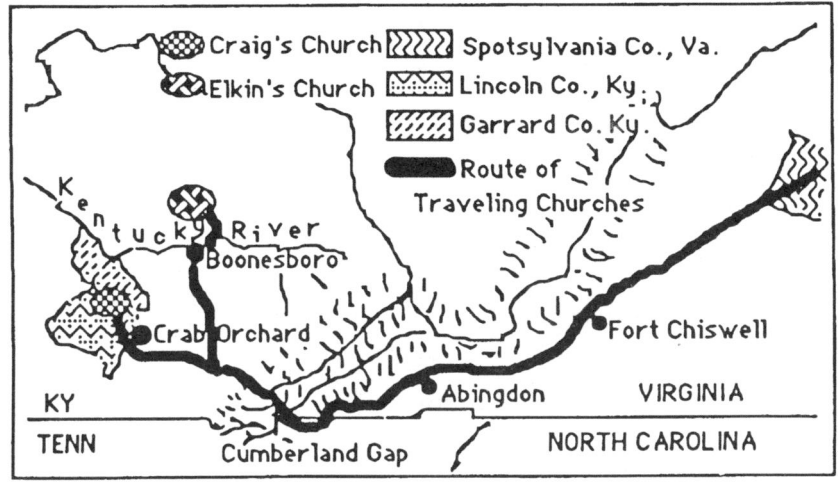

The Traveling Church of Lewis Craig arrived in Kentucky in 1781. That of Robert Elkin and Captain Billy Bush settled in 1783.

A monument marks the original site of Lewis Craig's Upper Spotsylvania Church, located within the perimeter of Chancellorsville Battle Field. Brigadier Gen. J.H. Wilson, on May 5, 1864, reported to headquarters that he had skirmished "heavily with the enemy's cavalry at and beyond Craig's Church." (*War of the Rebellion*, Series I, Vol. 36, Pt. 1, p. 871)

CHAPTER 4

STOCKTON'S VALLEY AND THE FORMATIVE YEARS (1796-1804)

The birth of John Smith in 1784 occurred three years following the end of the Revolutionary War and only nine years after Daniel Boone and his thirty axmen had hacked their way through Cumberland Gap.[1] The "Traveling Churches" of Lewis Craig and Robert Elkin had recently settled in Kentucky, and Barton Warren Stone, with whom Smith was destined to share a significant role in the Restoration Movement in Kentucky, was a lad of eleven years. It would be another four years before the birth of Alexander Campbell, the great scholar who would contribute immeasurably to the shaping of Smith's religious persuasion.

In the fall of 1795, eleven-year-old John Smith, his father, and an older brother traversed Cumberland Gap and traveled the Wilderness Road to Crab Orchard, Kentucky. They then took another trace south on their way to the edge of the rugged frontier to select a new dwelling place. Since the Wilderness Road did not open to wagon traffic until the fall of 1796, they journeyed by horseback while leading packhorses laden with a plow and other essentials for subduing the wild wilderness. It is likely that at least one of the three was on foot much of the time prodding along two or three cows which were necessary for their sustenance.

While the father and two of his sons were searching for an acceptable location, the remainder of the Smith family had been temporarily settled slightly east of the Gap in the relative security of the well traveled valley of the Powell River. Eventually selected was a boundary of two hundred acres of virgin wilderness in Stockton's Valley, an exceptionally fertile area located south of the Cumberland River and approximately three miles north of the Tennessee border.

This picturesque vale, threaded by pristine streams, was framed by the low lying crests and wooded slopes of Poplar Mountain.

Considering the fact that there were several trails to the Cumberland River area,[2] it is difficult to ascertain the reason for the route selected by George Smith for his trek to Stockton's Valley. The Wilderness Road to Crab Orchard and the southwest route traveled to Stockton's Valley were considerably farther than a more direct one to the West. There are two possibilities as to why the Wilderness Road route was chosen.

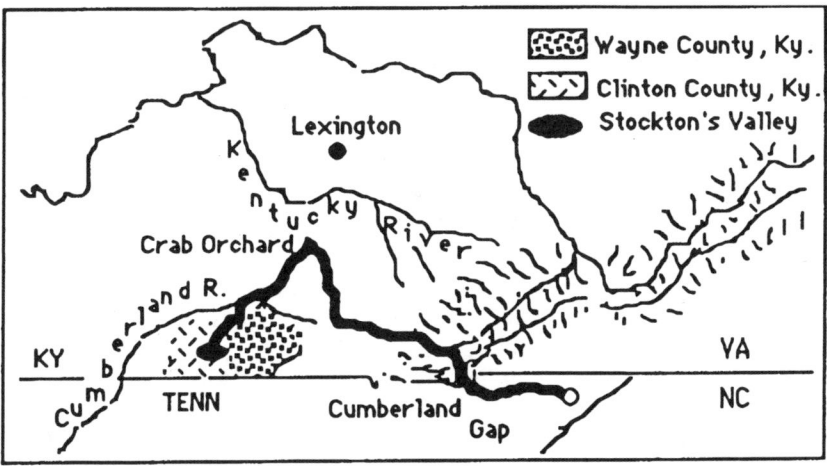

In the fall of 1795 George Smith, with sons Joseph and John, journeyed through Cumberland Gap, along the Wilderness Road to Crab Orchard, and southwest to Stockton's Valley.

First, there is the likelihood that Smith was not certain of his destination when he departed for the edge of the Kentucky frontier to claim a new location for his home. Perhaps he did not decide on the Cumberland River country until he arrived at Crab Orchard, the northern most point on his route. For more than a decade the fertile region of Central Kentucky had experienced a flood of pioneers clamoring for land. This could have persuaded him to seek his fortune on the less populated southwest portion of the frontier.

Second, assuming that Smith was relatively certain of his destination, perhaps the most decisive factor in the choice of route was the presence of hostile Indians on the more direct route from the Holston River country in East Tennessee. The Wilderness Road had been made safer from Indian attack after 1794, but the marauding

Chickamaugas, a renegade subtribe of the Cherokees, essentially controlled the South Fork of the Cumberland River area. The cruel and clever Doublehead, chief of the Chicamaugas, was the scourge of East Tennessee and Southern Kentucky for a score of years.[3]

It was not until 1805 that the South Fork country was secure from the Indian menace. In that year President Thomas Jefferson, determined to have a road built through the area, persuaded Chief Doublehead to enter into a treaty in which the Indians relinquished claim to the territory in return for another boundary in which their safety was guaranteed. The Cherokee tribe considered Doublehead's entering into such an agreement as an act of treason and three executioners were chosen to impose a sentence of death against him. In 1807, after two years of pursuit, the executioners accomplished their mission.[4]

Wisely, George Smith chose the inconvenience of the longer journey with fewer risks rather than the shorter route which entailed greater dangers for his large family. He knew well of the massacres of entire families enroute to new homes in the West.

Only one other settler had preceded George Smith into the valley in which he staked his claim. Thomas Stockton, from whom the valley derived its name, came from Albemarle County, Virginia, approximately three years prior to Smith's arrival.[5] The hardy old pioneer most likely was delighted to have neighbors to share in the taming of his portion of the West which often became very lonely.

When territory from western Wayne County, Kentucky and eastern Cumberland County was included in the formation of the county of Clinton in 1835, Stockton's Valley came within the bounds of the latter. Unfortunately, the historic name of Stockton eventually was replaced by Duvall Valley, yielding to a rather prolific family of that name. However, the name of Smith Creek, a stream traversing the valley from north to south, and on either side of which was located the original farm of George Smith, has survived to the present.[6]

In the spring of 1796 John and Joseph Smith were left by their father in the loneliness of the wilderness to care for the newly planted crops while he returned to Powell's Valley to accompany the remaining members of his family to their new home. In retrospect, it is perhaps impossible to perceive the depth of the apprehensions gripping the concerned father as he was faced with threats on two fronts. On the one was the matter of leaving two boys alone with a dangerous assignment, and on the other was the monumental task of moving his large family some two hundred miles along a hazardous route. Even though the Wilderness Road had become somewhat safer because of recent treaties with the Indians, sufficient risks still remained to compound his anxieties.

It was midsummer before the father returned to the valley with the remainder of the Smith family. The Wilderness Road pilgrims consisted of older family members driving livestock, the mother and small children on horseback with packhorses in tow, and boys old enough for the assignment carrying their trusted rifles and serving as guard and escort for the entire caravan. When the procession arrived in Stockton's Valley it was greeted with an exuberant shout from brother John, by now a seasoned twelve-year-old frontiersman.[7]

John Augustus Williams, the 1870 biographer of John Smith, records that George and Rebecca Smith were the parents of thirteen children.[8] According to the Smiths' genealogy, at the time their residence was established in Stockton's Valley there were nine boys and five girls ranging from twenty-six-year-old Philip down to two-year-old Henry. By this time, father George was sixty-four and mother Rebecca was fifty-five.[9] The fact that no deaths are recorded among the children during their early years is indicative of an exceptionally sturdy pioneer stock.

STOCKTON'S VALLEY
In the fall of 1795, George Smith staked a two-hundred-acre claim in Stockton's Valley, located in present-day Clinton County, Kentucky.

The apparent discrepancy between biographer and family genealogy may be explained by the assumption that Jesse, the fourth child listed in the table, was a foster child.[10] Remembering that the father of the Smith clan had received assistance from a compassionate family when he was left an orphan, George Smith's willingness to extend, in turn, the same type of care and concern to an unfortunate lad is indicative of an appreciative and benevolent disposition.

THE CRAB ORCHARD FIDDLER

One of the people who had much to do with the direction of John Smith's life was Jeremiah Vardeman, whom he had encountered shortly after arriving in Kentucky. Indeed, Vardeman was responsible for Smith's eventual move from Wayne to Montgomery County, which in turn resulted in the latter coming into contact with the Restoration Movement. Their first meeting was the result of an unusual combination of circumstances.

One evening in Stockton's Valley during the winter prior to the arrival of the remainder of the family, as George Smith sat with John and Joseph, he presented a monumental challenge to the younger of the two boys.

"John, we must have some bread, and soon we will need some corn to plant," advised the contemplative father. Apparently much time had been spent by George in pondering the necessary procedure for survival within the harsh environs of the wilderness.

"It is more than a hundred miles to Horine's mill," continued the father. "You are now twelve years old, and I know you are smart enough to make the trip. It will keep back the work too much for me or Joe to go. Suppose then, tomorrow you get ready the packhorses and start."

One can perceive that the young heart of John leaped with both expectation and excitement as the elder Smith directed him to "Follow the trace which leads north to Crab Orchard, and people there will tell you where to find the mill."

Without a thought of disobeying his father, in the spirit of Abraham when God instructed him to go to Mount Moriah and sacrifice Isaac, John was ready at sunrise the next morning to begin a journey which held numerous potential perils for a lad of only twelve. After a few hours of riding one horse and leading another equipped with a packsaddle, he stood on the southern bank of the treacherous Cumberland River then swollen by recent rains. With the assistance of an accommodating stranger he managed to cross the river in a canoe, his horses swimming along side.

After threading his way through the wilderness for another two or three days, John, cold and hungry, entered Crab Orchard, a frontier village strategically located on the Wilderness Road in Lincoln County. He would have immediately proceeded to the miller's house, but his attention was drawn in the direction of music flowing with the gentle evening breeze. Stepping to the cabin where the music originated, Smith peered through the crowd. His eyes came to rest upon the imposing personage of Jeremiah Vardeman, who was playing the fiddle for a dance.

The fiddler, by far the most conspicuous figure in the dance crowd, was described as being "a young man of fine face and form, and was dressed in a gay coat and yellow velvet breeches."[11] The party-loving Vardeman had only recently been dismissed from the Baptist Church because he had become associated with a dancing school. Colonel William Whitley had permitted the school to be conducted on the third floor of the "Guardian of the Wilderness Road," the designation of his fortress-like mansion which was located near Crab Orchard.

THE WILLIAM WHITLEY HOUSE
Colonel William Whitley constructed the first brick house in Kentucky. It became known as the "Guardian of the Wilderness Road."

Soon after John's first glimpse of the expert fiddle player, the latter was restored to the Baptist fold by the preaching of Thomas Hansford, an "unlettered" but respected preacher among Kentucky Baptists.[12] Fate, or perhaps providence, would bring Smith and Vardeman into contact many times during the first part of the approaching nineteenth century.

ANOTHER DANGEROUS ASSIGNMENT

Sometime during 1799 residents were gripped with fear when it was learned that the notorious Harpe gang, plague of the Wilderness Road and the frontier for several years, had entered Stockton's Valley and callously murdered two of Smith's neighbors. Folks in the area were well acquainted with the gang because two of the women who traveled with Micajah, or "Big Harpe," were daughters of Jesse Roberts, an early settler who had followed the Smiths into the valley.[13] Following the brutal crime, it was believed that the infamous gang had joined other fugitives in Logan County.

The county of Logan, considered to have been a part of a larger area known as the Green River country, had become known as "Rogues" Harbor. It had received this designation because murderers, horse thieves, robbers and counterfeiters had fled there from all parts of the country in an attempt to escape justice. Such a desperate situation led law abiding citizens to organize under the name of "Regulators" in an attempt to establish some semblance of law and order.[14]

Just prior to the Harpes' incursion into Stockton's Valley, George, the third son of the Smith family, married and moved west to the Green River country. Soon after, it was conjectured that the Harpes were in Logan County, and a report that brother George had become one of their victims reached Stockton's Valley.[15] The concerned father, in an attempt to learn more about the fate of George, turned to one of the older brothers and to fifteen-year-old John, who seemed to have a way of mastering difficult situations.

Arriving at their destination, the brothers learned that George had nonchalantly entered the camp of the Harpes, mistaking them to be peaceful hunters. It is very likely that George and the Roberts girls quickly recognized one another, since their parents were neighbors in Stockton's Valley. At any rate, the rogues seized him with the intent of taking his life.

While Big Harpe was attempting to hold a struggling George so that Little Harpe could aim for a fatal shot, a posse, which had been formed after a mother and her children had perished at the hands of the brutal pair, rode upon them during the struggle. Mistaken for one of the gang, George was shot in the leg by one of the pursuers. To the relief of peace-loving settlers, the Harpe brothers eventually met violent ends, similar to the type they had administered to an unknown number of innocent and unsuspecting victims.

After considerable difficulty with the wound he had received, George eventually regained his mobility and was as agile as ever. However, impressed with the safety of Stockton's valley, he requested his brothers to return during the summer and assist him in moving back near his family. While George resolved to spend the remainder of his days among his kindred,[16] young John had experienced another episode which continued to condition him for the life of a frontier preacher committed to risks and sacrifices in the interest of others.

A CALVINIST PREACHER AND A CONCERNED MOTHER

Young John Smith was a precocious youngster and appeared to be serious-minded most of the time. He was impressive in appearance, articulate in discussion, and endowed with a keen sense of humor. His love of nature was conducive to a natural adaptation to life on the frontier. However, he possessed a tendency to occasionally revel in the lighter side of life. Of him one author recorded:

> John Smith loved the wild, free existence he was permitted to have in Stockton's Valley. He spent much of his time exploring caves and rockshelters and hunting dear, bear and turkey with friendly Cherokee who frequently camped on his father's land. Tall and robust, with an aquiline [sic] nose and a shock of dark hair, John was an impressive figure of a young man, full of life and full of mischief, both the pride and the bane of his family.[17]

The "bane of his family" is not intended to imply that John was a constant source of concern, but rather that he was often unpredictable as to which course he would eventually take. Louis Cockran, the fictionalizing author of Smith's life, perhaps epitomized him accurately on one occasion when he portrayed him as saying, "I'm a contrary person and folks was just curious about what I would do next."[18] His parents felt that his mirthful disposition sometimes led him astray, but beyond some card playing and attending dances ·in the valley his sensitive conscience prevented him from becoming enmeshed in the grosser offenses of drunkenness, profanity, and gambling.[19]

For two years after the family of George Smith entered Stockton's Valley the settlers were without an organized church. In the absence of preachers on the frontier, families who were religiously inclined observed times of Bible reading and prayer either in their own homes or in the homes of neighbors. However, this arrangement soon changed for the families in Stockton's Valley.

When John Smith was fourteen years old, Isaac Denton, a Baptist preacher, moved into the area. In 1798 Denton received a two-hundred-acre land grant in the vicinity of Clear Fork Creek, a tributary of Spring Creek, which in turn emptied into Wolf River a short distance to the south. He organized a Baptist Church near the source of Clear Fork Creek, and soon a small building was constructed just over the ridge west of Stockton's Valley.[20]

The preacher made a significant impact upon the life of young John Smith. Denton was committed to orthodox Calvinism, taking seriously the predestination provisions of that particular doctrine. He saw much promise for John, and very much wanted him to become a preacher if it were determined that he was among the elect.

John regularly attended church services at Clear Fork Baptist Church, and because he entertained a special appreciation for the pious preacher, he often assisted the latter in working his corn field. Frequently, in search of some encouraging word pertaining to his own spiritual welfare, the curious youngster would probe the mind of the respected Denton. The concern that he could possibly be among the eternally damned received no alleviation from the staunch Calvinist preacher.

"You cannot truly repent of your sins, or believe in a Savior, till your whole moral nature has been changed by the power of the Holy Ghost," Denton would in effect inform the young disciple.

"And what must I do in order to have this change of which you speak wrought within me?" John would plead.

"Nothing, John," the old preacher would resolutely respond. "God's grace is sovereign and unconditional. If you are of his sheep, you will be called, and you will hear his voice and follow him."

"But when, Mr. Denton, will the Lord call?"

Consistently and without any deviation, the reply came: "In his own good time, John. He has marked out your whole life, and determined your destiny according to his own wise but hidden and eternal purpose."

In his desperation John turned to his beloved mother and pled with her, "As my best earthly friend, tell me what more I ought to do; for I would give the whole world to be a Christian."

"Ah, John," said she, with tears in her eyes, "you must wait the Lord's time."

"Mother," the son replied in despair, "I don't believe that the Lord's time will ever come; I shall die and be lost forever!"[21]

AMONG THE ELECT OF GOD

The perplexing apprehensions which gripped John Smith were nourished by his concerned mother. Neither did the steadfast Calvinist preacher diminish the desire of the serious-minded lad to escape the horrors of hell, nor did he lessen the hope of eternal life with the elect. During the meetings at Clear Fork Church John listened while others related experiences declared to be God's assurance that they were among the chosen of the Heavenly Father. Revivals sweeping the frontier at this time came to the Clear Fork Baptist Church, and with skepticism he watched the contortions of those with whom the spirit was supposed to be dealing.

At the time he had gone to assist George in his return to Stockton's Valley, John had encountered one of James McGready's revivals in Logan County. With feelings akin to disgust, he had witnessed the camp meeting. Looking upon the novel and extravagant scenes so foreign to what he deemed solemn and worshipful in nature, he was not certain whether he should feel amused or offended.[22]

Somehow, Smith had much difficulty in accepting something which appeared to be so contradictory to the nature of pure religion, but was declared to be scriptural by those who had instructed him. He ultimately resolved that he would examine the subject of salvation in the light of his "inspired reading book," feeling assured that what was to him so unreasonable would also be unscriptural. As he studied the Scriptures, he went through depths of despair, agonizing over his depraved condition.

Finally, after fervent prayers and intense emotional struggles, John, defying lingering reservations, chose to go before the church and relate his experiences. Afterwards, every hand was raised when the moderator requested of the assembly: "All who believe that the experience just related is a work of grace, hold up their right hand."[23] In 1804, at the age of twenty, John Smith was accepted "by experience" into membership of the Clear Fork Baptist Church.[24]

PEACE IN THE VALLEY—AND SADNESS

It can be assumed that in the Smith Homestead during the first few months in Stockton's Valley there was a beehive of activity among the older siblings—six sons wielding axes and three daughters helping with gardening and domestic chores. When the echo of the axes and falling timber ceased, the elder Smith could survey one of the most appealing stretches of land on the Kentucky frontier. Encircling his family table were fourteen children with whom he and Rebecca had survived difficult times. He and his devoted wife certainly must have felt a deep sense of satisfaction in what had been accomplished.

However, a change in the complexion of the family was imminent. Several of the older children were approaching the age when they would become interested in choosing mates and establishing homes of their own. Even though this type of transition is expected in any family, George Smith was entering a period which would require a series of adjustments unlike anything he had anticipated.

The first breach in the closely knit family occurred with the marriage of George, his namesake. Having imbibed the frontier spirit of his father, he chose to move farther west.

The second disruption came in 1798 when the oldest son, Philip, claimed a wife. Soon thereafter, Rebecca, the Smith's firstborn daughter and namesake of her mother, wed Jessie Stockton, son of their first neighbor in Stockton's Valley.

A one-year reprieve on weddings was broken in 1801 when a double wedding occurred in the family. On October 15th of that year sons Joseph and William married sisters Susannah and Margaret Ryder. Since every opportunity to break the boredom and drudgery in the wilderness was seized upon, brothers marrying sisters provided an occasion for much celebration. Most likely the exuberance presented brother James, the fiddle player in the Smith family, an incentive to play his popular frontier instrument with an extra measure of vigor.

During the first five years after the marriage of the first son, their married children presented to George and Rebecca at least nine grandchildren. As their spiritual-minded parents had done, the children continued the practice of frequently assigning Bible names to their offspring. Perhaps a high point during these years was the birth of twin daughters to their son George in 1798. The little girls received the names of Rose and Sharon, a clever adaptation of the appealing "Rose of Sharon" of the Scriptures.

In 1801 the Smith parents were destined for a period of deep grief, the first of its kind to be experienced in their large family. Two days after the weddings of Joseph and William twenty-three-year-old James, the family musician, "signed on" as a poleman on the *Natchez Belle*. It is not known at what point James boarded the boat, whose cargo was tobacco and hemp, but its destination was New Orleans. The family never heard from James again.

Evidence appears to suggest that John and James were much alike in temperament, in that they were the most jovial members in the family. It is believed that James often entertained on special occasions, and to the chagrin of father George, John called the sets while James played the fiddle at neighborhood square dances. Mother Rebecca tacitly approved, believing that the activity was healthy for the energetic young people.[25]

The marriage of the older sons and the loss of James left seventeen-year-old John as the oldest son remaining at home with his aging parents. Also residing at home were two brothers and two sisters younger than he and perhaps as many as three unmarried sisters who were older. Consequently, in addition to sustained grief because of the loss of his brother, young John was laden with heavy responsibility.

THE DEATH OF A PATRIARCH

In the latter part of 1803 John Smith's father was seized with a lingering illness. When it was evident that the elder Smith was not responding to the treatment of herbs from the forest and the best of other home remedies, he called John and solemnly charged:

> And now I know, my boy, that a heavy burden will rest on your young shoulders; but do right, and the Lord, to whose care I commend you, will give you wisdom, and bless you in your undertakings.[26]

Since sailing with his parents from Germany to America while yet a baby, George Smith, over the course of his life, had been a part of three frontiers. As his life ebbed away, his mind was perhaps flooded with vivid memories of the back-country of Virginia, the Holston River Valley, and the taming of a portion of the rugged Kentucky wilderness.

Many significant events and eras had transpired during Smith's eventful life. The young country for which he had fought had established itself as an independent nation. His beloved Kentucky, no longer a county of the Old Dominion, had become a sovereign state in 1792. As he remembered the years of religious oppression in Virginia, it must have been satisfying to know that the freedom-loving Thomas Jefferson, one of the champions of religious liberty, had been elected the president of the young Republic.

Among his last requests was that John, nineteen years of age, take charge of the farm until his two younger brothers, Jonathan and Henry, ages sixteen and ten,[27] were old enough to assume the responsibility of managing the farm and of caring for their mother.

Unfortunately, George Smith did not live long enough to be assured that John was safely within the fold of God's elect. Of comfort to him, however, was the presence of a devoted wife and thirteen children who stood nearby as the seasoned old pioneer began his departure for yet another frontier. On March 20, 1804, seven brief years after moving his family to Stockton's Valley, the patriarch of the Smith family died at the age of seventy-two.

SMITH CREEK
Smith Creek serves as the only reminder that George Smith once lived in Stockton's Valley.

CHAPTER 5

ALONG THE LITTLE SOUTH FORK
(1805-1814)

At the time of his father's death in 1804 John Smith's primary responsibility involved caring for his widowed mother and two sisters who were younger than he. The sisters, Fanny Mae and Jane, were twelve and fourteen respectively.[1] Approximately one year later, apparently believing that brothers Jonathan and Henry were sufficiently mature to assume the domestic mantle, John chose to venture twenty miles east to Horse Hollow. William, a brother three years older than he, had recently acquired land in that vicinity.[2]

A current aerial view of a portion of southeastern Wayne County presents in vivid detail the area of Horse Hollow and the contiguous landscape along the Little South Fork of the Cumberland River. The area under consideration begins near the base of Mt. Piscah and extends approximately four miles in a northeasterly direction parallel with the north bank of the Little South Fork. The cleared land, outlined by the wooded section, resembles the body of a mythical dragon.

At a point where the Little South Fork makes an abrupt turn toward the east, Horse Hollow begins forming the dragon's neck. Pitching backwards toward the north for the first mile, then curving to the northeast, the two cleared forks at the head of the hollow form the nostrils and lower jaw of the imaginary head. The bowed neck and the open mouth present the image of the vicious beast poised to devour its prey.

The hollow averages only about one-fourth mile in width as it stretches approximately two miles before it abruptly ends. No outlet exists except a barely discernible trail which, on occasions, has been used by loggers. Accessibility from the east to Horse Hollow is limited because the Daniel Boone National Forest begins at the Little South

Fork and extends eastward over the Cumberland Plateau. Paradoxically, the oldest settlement in Wayne County is believed to have been established in this seemingly remote valley.

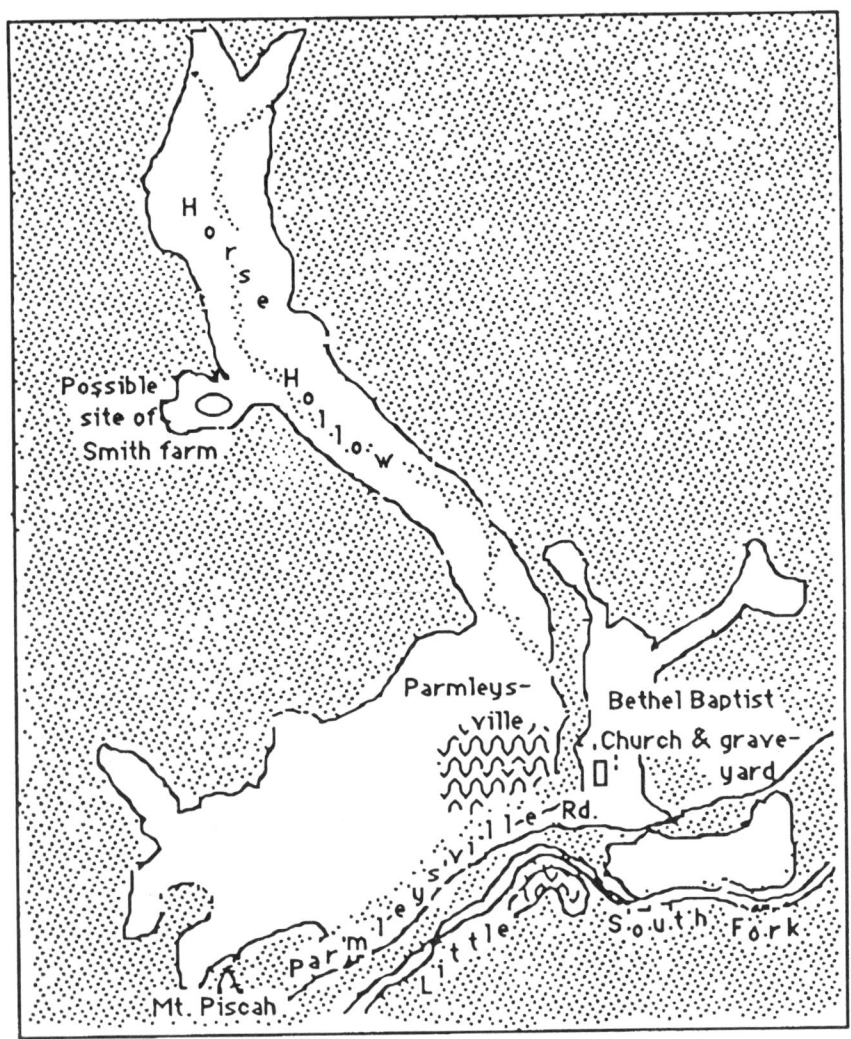

LITTLE SOUTH FORK REGION
The above is a sketch of the Little South Fork and Parmleysville area. Horse Hollow is approximately two miles in length and less than one-fourth mile in width.

It is generally accepted that Horse Hollow, sometime before its cession by the Indians, derived its name from the practice of horse thieves hiding their stolen animals in the secluded area. Following the horse thief era, perhaps as early as the 1780's, settlers entered the region by way of the rugged Southern Ridge Trail and established a settlement at the mouth of Horse Hollow. This date compares favorably with the earliest settlements in other sections of Kentucky considered much less remote.

It is believed that the first white settlers along the Little South Fork and in Horse Hollow had been citizens of the aborted State of Franklin, the same area from which the George Smith family had departed. Disconcerted with what was considered unfair treatment at the hands of North Carolina, some chose to move to the protection of a fort constructed by Robert Parmley, who was born and reared within the bounds of Franklin. In its early years the settlement, named Parmleysville in honor of its founder, was well populated by Parmleys, inasmuch as Robert was the husband of two wives and the father of twenty-two children.[3]

From a description of the location of Parmleysville and Horse Hollow one would perhaps surmise that the area was rather isolated. However, various trails crisscrossed the vicinity of both the South Fork and the Little South Fork of the Cumberland and gave access to the Old Tellico Trace Indian Trail located a short distance east of Parmleysville. That trail, which eventually became known as the Jacksboro Road sometime after 1808, constituted the main route from Danville, Kentucky, through Jacksboro, Tennessee, and finally terminated at the Tennessee River.

Parmleysville was also accessible from the southwest. Travelers using that route entered Wayne County from the north where a trail departed The Tellico Trace near Tateville. After pursuing the route into Monticello, those destined for Parmleysville followed a southeastward course up Beaver Creek to Mt. Piscah, and continued northeastward down the valley of the Little South Fork.[4]

Parmleysville was early noted for its race track and fine horses. This particular feature of the frontier village attracted frequent visitors to the region. It was characterized by a steady population growth, rivaling Monticello in attempting to become the seat of government when Wayne became an organized county in 1800.[5]

A view across the site of old Parmleysville. Bethel Baptist Church can be seen through the trees in the background. The road, which winds its way up Horse Hollow, is visible to the left.

A LAND PURCHASE IN HORSE HOLLOW

Settlement along the Little South Fork received added impetus after 1805, the year the Cherokee Indians deeded the area to the United States government. With the land becoming available for official surveying and patenting, twenty-one-year-old John Smith managed to acquire two hundred acres in Horse Hollow.[6] Since the hollow has the capacity of yielding only three hundred total acres of tillable land, much of his acreage was composed of woodland extending up and beyond the hills which framed the valley. Regardless of the limited amount of tillable land, with the fifty-dollar purchase John had established for himself a measure of independence which he had not previously known.

At the turn of the nineteenth century Parmleysville had no rival in terms of features which would attract enterprising young men. It can be conjectured, therefore, that young John was exceptionally pleased to have made a land purchase near the thriving frontier village. Perhaps of special appeal was the fact that the Little South Fork had been dammed to provide power for a grist mill,[7] an installation of significance to John since he certainly remembered traveling one hundred miles nine years earlier for the benefits of such a luxury.

Very soon after the purchase of the land, and as soon as he could make necessary arrangements for Jonathan and Henry to continue operating the family farm in Stockton's Valley, John moved to Horse Hollow. The only improvement on the land was an unfinished log cabin, hastily constructed by the previous owner who had acquired title to it by "headright."[8] This kind of possession simply required the construction of a cabin and living on the premises for one year.

LITTLE SOUTH FORK
The Little South Fork is shown at the point where it takes its eastward direction slightly west of Bethel Baptist Church and at the mouth of Horse Hollow. It is a tributary of the Big South Fork of the Cumberland River.

KNOWLEDGE BOUGHT IN THE MARKET

Soon after going to Horse Hollow, John's attention was temporarily diverted from the development of his farm when he learned that a teacher of repute had established a school in Stockton's

Valley. Seized by his drive to acquire an education, he hastily suspended his interests in Horse Hollow and returned home.

John discovered that Robert Ferrill's capability as a teacher was enhanced by his collection of good books. A mature and industrious man, Ferrill was by trade a wheelwright and a teacher by avocation. John walked almost four miles to school each day, and with the exuberance of a child the twenty-one-year-old student was regularly at his place of learning at the appointed time. However, disappointment soon came when the school closed because the demand on Ferrill for the making and repairing of wheels became greater than that for instruction.

Fortunately, Ferrill was so impressed with John's insatiable thirst for knowledge that he invited his ambitious student to come and live with him and engage in independent study in his library. John moved into Ferrill's shop with the understanding that the wheelwright would permit him to earn his support. He toiled either in the field or in the shop during the day, and at night gave attention to his studies by the blaze of the open fireplace.[9]

At this point in his life the determination of John Smith to improve his lot by way of an education was akin to other rare, gifted, and ambitious young men on the frontier. Five years after John began studying by the fire light in Robert Ferrill's shop, fifty miles northwest of Stockton's Valley in a cabin much like Smith's own Horse Hollow structure Abraham Lincoln was born. As a youth he likewise struggled in the field or split rails during the daylight hours and studied by the light of the fireplace at night.

It has been observed that "Grace is given of God, but knowledge is bought in the market."[10] It is difficult to identify that certain quality which drove a Smith and a Lincoln to the marketplace and the subsequent tough bargaining process necessary to acquire their knowledge, but the formative years of Smith and Lincoln were certainly similar. The harsh frontier with its drought of opportunities occasionally brought forth such giants who shaped the destiny of multitudes.

HOME IN HORSE HOLLOW

At a point when John felt that to continue pursuing his studies in the home of the compassionate Ferrill would be taking unfair advantage, he chose once again to depart Stockton's Valley. He arranged the affairs of the family farm one more time so that his widowed mother could survive with his younger brothers and sisters, then returned to Horse Hollow. Rather than live alone in the primitive cabin on his own farm, he chose to continue for a time in the home of his brother.[11]

This second departure from Stockton's Valley was a turning point for John. With the exception of an occasional visit, he never again resided in the environs of his boyhood home. The old farm of George Smith was left to Jonathan and Henry as compensation for caring for Rebecca Smith, who at this time was sixty-four years old.[12]

When John returned to the hollow, after having studied under Robert Ferrill, he had attained additional stature among the residents. Still lingering was the spiritual warmth kindled by the great revivals which had recently swept Kentucky. Neighbors, who for the most part were Baptists, frequently met in cabins for periods of singing and praying, and in the absence of an ordained preacher, someone with a "natural gift" was encouraged to "exhort."

John eventually became fluent in praying and singing, but at first was reluctant to exhort at the social meetings. However, with the persistence of his friends, he eventually agreed to do so. Taking seriously the added responsibility, he spent much time in preparation. His first experience at exhorting was of such nature that many years later he remembered it in vivid detail.

He related that after the usual period of singing and praying he arose with confidence to speak his words of exhortation. Once on his feet, however, he was startled to discover that his mind had relinquished its treasures. The silence was torture as he gazed at the faces of those who composed the audience. When his thoughts refused to return, on an impulse, he rushed for the door and dashed out into the night.

Young Smith's hasty departure was abruptly terminated when his foot, with much force, struck an unknown solid object and he was thrown to the ground. When he managed to arise, to his delight his thoughts had returned with clarity and distinctness just as suddenly as they had made their departure. Feeling that he could now deliver the exhortation, he returned to the house and spoke with the fervency of one who had been touched by inspiration.

It was at one of these social meetings that John's attention was arrested by the charm of Anne Townsend. Very soon after being impressed by the prospects of her becoming his wife, he approached her father and inquired about submitting a proposal to Anne.[13]

In his fictional account of "The Wooing" Louis Cochran perhaps accurately captured the apprehension of Anne's father and the awkwardness of the country boy who sought his daughter's hand.

"You been doing some exhorting," the father began abruptly. "Do you aim to be a preacher or a farmer? Not that I got anything against preachers; give or take a little, they're as good as most. But a preacher is generally a poor provider for his family, and Anne's given to good living. She's not used to working much in the fields."

"I'll always be a farmer," John replied as he shifted awkwardly. "But I might take to preaching, too. I don't know. I'll have to wait and see if the Lord calls me."

Townsend stared in disdain and declared, "I don't follow that line of talk. To my notion, a man's a free-will agent; he makes up his own mind."

With a puzzled countenance he scanned John and continued, "Us Townsends ain't church members. Why should you be wanting a wife who wouldn't be yoked with you in your thinking?"

"I could convert her," countered John courageously. "Leastways, I'd try. I wouldn't want to risk losing my wife in eternity."

"It'd take a lot of doing," Townsend chortled. "Anne is given to reasoning things out like me; she puts no store in waiting on miracles." [14]

Even though he considered himself unskilled in the art of courtship, John's sincere manner and untarnished character soon won the heart of Anne. On December 9, 1806, he married the first and only girl he had ever loved.[15]

Twenty-two-year-old John immediately moved his twenty-year-old bride[16] to his humble Horse Hollow cabin. Assisted by his enthusiastic companion, he transformed the crude structure so that it soon compared favorably with others in the Hollow and along the Little South Fork. The couple did not differ from their neighbors, inasmuch as all were accustomed to the deprivations and toil which accompanied life on the frontier.

Their daily lives consisted of clearing the land and cultivating the fields with the crude tools of the day. To sustain themselves, however, it was necessary to also invade the forest for its wild fruit, herbs, and game, as well as claim whatever the streams could yield. Flora and fauna of the Little South Fork and Horse Hollow flourished and John had learned how to reap the greatest harvest from their bounty. He knew the ways of the clever raccoon and kept on hand dogs used in the hunting of bear and other large game. The region was also enhanced by saltpeter caves whose valuable minerals were so essential for the preservation of meat and for the explosive necessary to assist in igniting gunpowder for the frontier muzzle loader.[17]

ORDAINED TO PREACH

By the time of his marriage John had been thrust by his religious neighbors into the leadership role at the social gatherings. He nurtured his own religious zeal, and even though exceedingly busy developing his farm, he encouraged frequent social meetings. Anne remained among the unconverted, but evidence suggests that she was interested in matters pertaining to her soul and in the spiritual aspirations of her husband.

John Smith very much desired to become a preacher. Richard Barrier, the ordained minister who was appointed to watch over the faithful at Parmleysville, recognized John's qualifications for the ministry and recommended that he be given liberty to "improve his gifts." Knowing that his brethren would soon be insisting upon his ordination, John became very troubled because the call from above had not come and he had no assurance that it ever would.

The respected young religious leader of Horse Hollow began diligently probing within, and observing from without, for any unusual event or apparent supernatural transaction which could be interpreted as a sign from above. Beyond any earthly aspiration he longed for the approval of heaven in his desire to proclaim the eternal word which he had come so much to love. On one occasion he pondered whether a rattlesnake which, instead of striking him refrained as though charmed, might possibly be that call. Again, his narrow escape from a vicious bull was interpreted as possibly the extraordinary message from on high for which he sought.[18] John's waiting for the omen to preach was as elusive for him as his conversion experience had been four years earlier in Stockton's Valley.

Even in the absence of John's capacity to relate a clear, identifiable miraculous call to preach, his fellow Baptists continued to insist upon his ordination. John eventually yielded to their wishes and on the third Saturday in May, 1808, presbyters of the Stockton's Valley Baptist Association came to Parmleysville to preside over the ordination of the twenty-four-year-old candidate.

"We suppose, brother Smith," one asked, "that you are well acquainted with the Philadelphia Confession of Faith?"

"I am well acquainted with it, brethren," replied the candidate.

"Do you adopt the articles therein set forth?"

"I do," replied the most respected of all young men who resided along the Little South Fork or in Horse Hollow.

When it was known in Stockton's Valley and among the Clear Fork Baptist Church membership that John was preaching, there was concern that he might possibly have been presumptuous about a call to preach. Philip Smith, the oldest brother of John, was sent to Parmleysville to ascertain the genuineness of the latter's heavenly anointment. Upon returning to Clear Fork, Philip assured his apprehensive brethren that indeed the Lord was with their favored son and that his younger brother should be permitted to continue with his divine mission.[19]

At an appropriate time John persuaded his brethren that there was a need for being formally organized into a church. Smith's biographer indicates that Isaac Denton was invited to officiate in the constitution of Bethel Baptist Church at Parmleysville. If that be the fact of the matter, the old Calvinist of Clear Fork certainly must have attended with delight since he had very much hoped that his youthful disciple was destined for the pulpit.[20]

The official record of the church, however, makes no mention of Denton being in attendance. It is possible that he came by invitation and participated in the ceremony, but apparently others were in charge. The minutes state:

> The Baptist Church of Christ on the Little South Fork by the name of Bethel was constituted on the Third Saturday in July, 1810, by a presbatry [sic] called for that purpose by Richard Barrier and Isham Burnett and was constituted on the principles of the union and was constituted on nine members to wit—John Parmley and his wife, Philip Smith and his wife, Roland Burnett, Jonathan Blevins, John Smith, Esther Koger, Stephen Vaughn. The next day Sister Nancy Burnett join [sic] by Letter.[21]

It is rather sad to note that Anne Townsend Smith is not listed among the membership. Four years after her marriage to John she was apparently still unable to relate an experience as evidence that she was among the elect. As much as he might have desired to intervene in her religious struggles, the doctrine of Calvinism prohibited John from interfering in such a private matter as the waiting of an apprehensive soul for the Holy Spirit to instill faith within the heart of one of the elect. These were difficult times for the young couple.

Approximately two months after the formal organization of the church, twenty-six-year-old John was chosen as her minister. The minutes continue:

> On September 16, 1810, the church met and chose Bro. John Smith as her first pastor and Bro. Philip Smith, his brother, as deacon and clerk.[22]

When Philip Smith visited his brother on behalf of the Clear Fork Baptists, he apparently was impressed with both the preaching of John and with the Little South Fork region. As indicated by the above entry he soon moved to the area of Parmleysville and became active in the newly organized church. No satisfactory reason exists for the exclusion of William Smith as a charter member other than his not having been the recipient of a miraculous experience. It will be remembered that he had preceded John to Horse Hollow.

As best as can be ascertained, the zealous group of Baptists at Parmleysville built a house of worship during the same year in which they were formally organized. To accommodate the construction of the house of worship, old Robert Parmley, although not mentioned among the early membership, contributed a choice plot of land overlooking the confluence of Horse Hollow with the Little South Fork.[23] Perhaps he felt the need to have his twenty-two children exposed to the type of climate which would emanate from Bethel Baptist Church.

After his ordination Smith's zeal knew no restraint. He pursued a full schedule of preaching both in and away from Parmleysville. Many years later as an old man he related that he:

> spent every moment that he could spare in the close and earnest study of his Bible, and the doctrines of his church, as they were set forth in the Confession of Faith. The pine-knots blazed on his hearth till a late hour every night; for he poured over the sacred text with a diligence that never tired. He saved the hour of noon, by reading while his tired yoke browsed in the shade or stood at the rick. He laid the Bible by his side on the dinner table, and committed to memory, over his plate, some verse on which he could ponder while at work. For he studied even in the fields, improvising sermons as he piled up his log heaps, and exhorting imaginary congregations as he plowed.[24]

As John Smith "poured [sic] over the sacred text" and the "doctrines of his church," little did he realize that a decade later he would experience painful conflicts because of their incompatibility. His profound respect for the Bible ultimately led him away from the Philadelphia Confession of Faith and into the flow of the movement to restore the New Testament order of the first century.

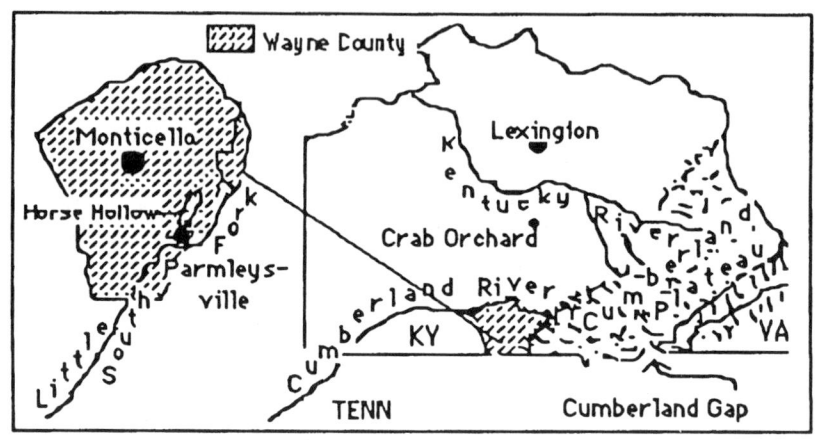

Horse Hollow is fifteen miles east of Stockton's Valley and situated at the base of the Cumberland Plateau. Parmleysville, a thriving early frontier settlement, was located at a point where the Little South Fork of the Cumberland River made an abrupt turn to the east.

BETHEL BAPTIST CHURCH

CHAPTER 6

THE DARKEST HOUR
(1814-1815)

UNFORGETTABLE JEREMIAH VARDEMAN

When twenty-six-year-old John Smith became the minister of Bethel Baptist Church at Parmleysville in 1810, he and Anne were the parents of two children. Eli, their firstborn, was approaching his second birthday and little Elvira was three months old.¹ The most popular couple in the Parmleysville area was exceptionally busy as they attempted to exact from the farm sustenance for their family, while at the same time remain heavily involved with the church.

The conscientious young preacher did not confine his preaching to the region of the Little South Fork. In addition to attending the meetings of the association of churches, of which Bethel Baptist Church was a member, he frequently preached at congregations other than Bethel. His interest in the world beyond the Little South Fork brought him into contact with some of the most influential preachers on the frontier. Among them was Jeremiah Vardeman.

Smith's second encounter with Vardeman occurred in 1810 at the annual meeting of the Cumberland River Baptist Association. It had been approximately fifteen years since he, as a twelve-year-old lad, had made the journey to Crab Orchard to purchase corn. The impressive three-hundred-pound former fiddle player had been oblivious to the youth's presence on the first occasion, but the second meeting was quite different.

Vardeman began preaching at Crab Orchard after being accepted back into the church and soon became the best known Baptist preacher in Kentucky. He had heard of Smith and knew of the effective work of the country preacher from Horse Hollow. Vardeman, who was nine years Smith's senior, quickly became aware

59

of the young preacher's potential and immediately began encouraging him to seek an area where he would be of greater usefulness to the church.

A VISION BEYOND HORSE HOLLOW

After a period of reluctance Smith slowly yielded to the admonitions of Vardeman. He made a visit to central Kentucky where Vardeman was preaching for churches in Fayette and Montgomery Counties. Even though impressed with the reception he received, he felt unprepared at that particular time for an assignment to that relatively affluent region.

The young preacher's consideration to move from the friendly environs of the Little South Fork was prompted by two concerns. First, he envisioned providing opportunities for his children beyond those he had been afforded. Second, he desired an arrangement beyond the provisions supplied by his Horse Hollow farm to sustain him and his family while he committed himself to his first love of studying the Bible and proclaiming its eternal message.[2]

Because Baptists in Virginia had been victims of the despised practice of supporting the clergy by taxation, and had observed the consequences of such an ecclesiastical system, they were essentially opposed to monetary support for preachers. In fact, many of the preachers were repulsed at the thought of accepting money for the proclamation of the mercy and grace of God. John Smith conscientiously shared their sentiments. Indeed, such a practice was among the reasons which had encouraged his beloved father and mother to depart the Old Dominion.

Because of this reaction, preachers on the rugged Kentucky frontier often sacrificed immeasurably in performing what they believed was a divine appointment. Representative of the sentiment which prevailed was an incident in the experiences of Elijah Barnes, a zealous elderly preacher who is credited with having organized the Grassy Lick Baptist Church in Montgomery County.

It is related that the gentle-hearted old minister was very poor, both "in spirit and in purse," and exceedingly humble in his demeanor before God and man. After leaving Montgomery and living in a crude cabin located on rocky hills which produced very little, he was overcome by desperate circumstances. Beyond a small family he could claim nothing except "Old Gray," his faithful horse which he rode on his monthly circuit.

During a severe drought both master and beast were near starvation. On one occasion, after the sermon had been completed, a concerned brother was convinced that the congregation should render some special assistance to their preacher. Having observed the leanness of the preacher's horse, the protagonist submitted to the congregation that if any present could spare a little meal or corn, he should send it to brother Barnes' family. The advocate enforced his appeal by noting the faithfulness of their devoted preacher for many years, while explaining that nothing had ever been contributed to his support.

While the old minister sat nearby, apologetically covering his face with his brawny hands, the proposition was immediately opposed by another member of the congregation. He argued that the Lord never taxed his children to support the gospel and that such a practice of rewarding preachers was "apt to puff them up with pride." The supporting brother, in behalf of their destitute minister, countered by quoting that "they who preach the gospel should live by the gospel."

"To live by the gospel is to live on the sweet and heavenly feelings which the gospel produces," insisted the antagonist. "On these divine things the preacher ought to feed."

His endurance expended, the old preacher suddenly sat erect and asked, "But what is Old Gray to do, my brother? He can't live on them sort of feelins."[3]

Because there was very little monetary compensation, some areas practiced "in kind" remuneration. Such was the case at the South Elkhorn Church located near Lexington, Kentucky. During the year of 1798, in behalf of John Shackleford, their minister, fourteen men submitted "subscriptions as a compensation for his services in the ministry in the bounds of South Elkhorn congregation." In addition to stipulations of money contributed by five of the fourteen, the remainder committed twelve and one-half pounds of salt, one barrel of corn and two of wheat, three hundred sixty-three pounds of pork, one hundred pounds of flour, one hundred pounds of beef, some sugar and tallow and thirty-six gallons of whiskey. He was perhaps one of the best paid and happiest preachers of that day.[4]

Fully aware of the sacrifices entailed in preaching, John Smith perceived his future as being more similar to that of Elijah Barnes than to that of the more affluent John Shackleford of South Elkhorn. Therefore, he could not be oblivious to the needs of his family as he gave himself more and more to preaching. His desire to preach with the possible deprivation of his family as a consequence ultimately led to a monumental decision.

A CLIMATE RIPE FOR SPECULATION

Complementing the influence of Vardeman were events on the national and international scenes which set in motion currents contributing to Smith's subsequent direction. Concurrent with Smith's becoming the preacher at Parmleysville was the election to Congress, in 1810-11, of several young members representing a new generation of Americans who had grown to maturity since the Revolutionary War. Among them were thirty-four-year-old Henry Clay and Richard M. Johnson of Kentucky, and John C. Calhoun of South Carolina. They were members of a group dubbed the "War Hawks" by John Randolph of Virginia.

Clay, who was later to become an acquaintance of Smith, quickly attained stature in the new Congress. After being elected Speaker of the House, he further strengthened his position by naming many of his friends as chairmen of important committees. Feeling that going to war was necessary for the national pride, the war hawks chose to abandon diplomatic channels, and in 1812 war was declared on Great Britain.

The reasons given for the declaration of the War of 1812 in actuality were not the legitimate ones leading to the conflict. Impressment of seamen and the failure to respect America's neutrality during a war in progress at the time between Britain and France were reasons given to appeal to those not supporting the war effort. Westerners, however, whom Henry Clay represented, supported the war with Britain for two additional reasons. First, they desired to move into Canada and claim some of her rich farm lands, and second, they believed that Britain was perhaps responsible for Tecumseh's attempt to organize a confederacy of Indian nations to resist the encroachment of land hungry pioneers in the old Northwest.[5]

The war dragged on for two years and nothing of substance was accomplished. In August of 1814, even though hostilities were continuing on the American continent, negotiations for the war's end began in the Flemish city of Ghent. The apparent imminent end to the war gave rise to speculation on the part of would-be entrepreneurs as to how best to take economic advantage of the aftermath of war. Within this context the enterprising John Smith sought for a possible arrangement which would permit him to be financially solvent while he preached with either very little or no compensation.

As Smith pondered these matters, he received information, apparently from friends and relatives, that land speculation in

Alabama would offer possibilities of making a fortune once the war was concluded.[6] A historical marker installed by the "Alabama Historical Associates" in New Market, Alabama, supports the fact that activity which would be associated with a newly settled area was indeed in progress during that time. The inscription on the marker states:

> Settled by pioneers early in 1806. George Smith, major landowner of town site, built log house and established mercantile business, 1814. John Miller excavated millrace, erected grist-mill and sawmill, 1819.

Since George Smith, the father of John, was orphaned while a small child, the name on the marker was likely not a relative. As will subsequently be revealed, the Miller family became closely associated with the Smiths.

A TRAGIC VENTURE

Before abruptly moving his family, Smith traveled to Alabama to explore the area under consideration. What he had heard was confirmed, in that lands once under Indian control were being offered for sale. The extreme northeast section of Alabama which he visited promised the possibility of realizing his dream of affluence.

In September of 1814, the month during which the British were bombarding Fort McHenry in Baltimore Harbor and Francis Scott Key was composing "The Star-Spangled Banner,"[7] John Smith was in the process of moving his wife and four children to Alabama. In addition to Eli and Elvira, who were seven and five years respectively, were two-year-old Jennie and four-month-old Zerelda.[8] The total entourage numbered eight, inasmuch as Anne's younger brother and sister accompanied them to assist in the chores associated with the move. Their destination was approximately one hundred fifty miles from Parmleysville.

On November 2, 1814, the Smiths were at Hickory Flats,[9] a part of which is included within the little community of present day Plevna, in Alabama's Madison County. Plevna is located two miles south of the Tennessee border and three miles north and slightly east of New Market, Alabama.[10]

The month of Smith's first visit to Alabama in 1814 is unknown. Of interest, however, is a record which asserts that on April 30, 1814, in the northeast quadrant of section four, one hundred fifty-nine and eighty-two hundredths acres were purchased by a John Smith and confirmed by certificate number 1131. Granting the possibility that the reference was to another John Smith, the fact remains that the location of the property was within the Hickory Flats area.

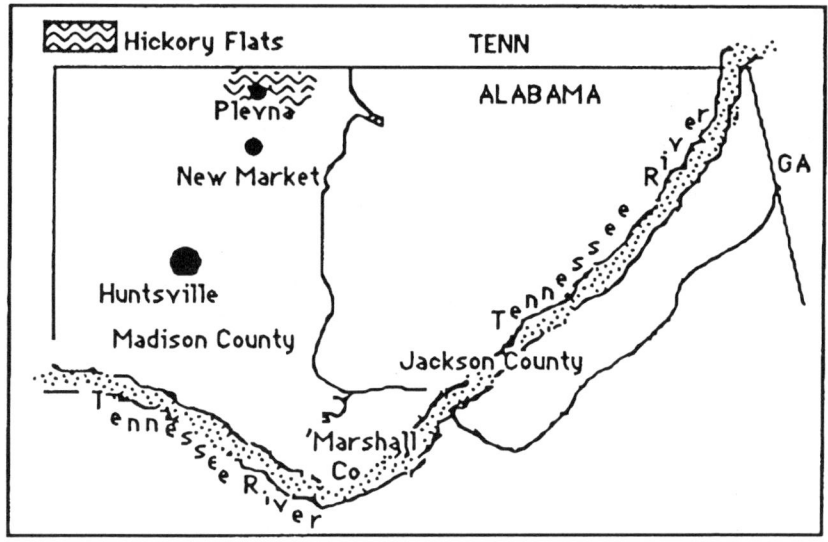

HICKORY FLATS

Hickory Flats, a name which no longer appears on current maps, is located in Madison County, Alabama. The Smiths settled approximately two miles south of the Tennessee River.

The prognosis that handsome profits could be made in land speculation proved to be sound. Good land selling in 1814 for one dollar and twenty-five cents per acre had soared into the twenty to fifty-dollar range by 1817. Some of the most fertile soil was priced for as much as one hundred dollars per acre by 1818.[11]

The escalating land prices were exactly that for which thirty-one-year-old John Smith had hoped. Conditions were right for him to reap windfall profits from the buying and selling of land. To enhance the situation, he had in his possession enough money from the sale of his Horse Hollow farm to purchase several hundred acres.

Conditions on the national and international scenes were also promising. The Treaty of Ghent, which officially ended the war, was signed on December 24, 1814. General Andrew Jackson, not knowing of the provisions to cease hostilities, was preparing to battle the

The Darkest Hour

British at New Orleans. Even though occurring after the war's end, Old Hickory's rout of the British proved politically advantageous in that it left him, in the eyes of a grateful nation, the greatest hero of the war.[12]

Tragically, the huge profits in land speculation at the war's end were to be realized by those other than the young enterprising preacher. Approximately two months after arriving at Hickory Flats, John was invited to go fifteen or twenty miles distance to preach in an area where some friends of the Smith family had relocated. In his absence the most dreaded disaster struck.

At dawn on January 7, 1815, two messengers appeared at the door of the residence in which John had lodged for the night. "Mr. Smith," they reluctantly informed him, "we are sorry to bring bad news from home. Your house took fire last night, and everything is lost. Two of the children were burned to death!"

"O God!" cried the stricken father, and his head dropped upon his breast.

The cabin had become engulfed in flames while Anne, his wife, was away attending an ill neighbor. She had taken the youngest daughter with her while her brother and sister were at home with the remaining three children. Two-year-old Jennie was rescued by her aunt who was in bed with her.

How to address Anne in her deep grief was John's piercing concern as he hurried home.

"I can give her no consolation!" he thought. "If I tell her that our babies are glorified, the thought that possibly they were among the non-elect will only aggravate her woe."

The grieving husband dreaded viewing his wife in her anguish and hearing her ask, "Are our children among the elect of God?"

In his desperation he attempted to persuade himself that non-elect persons do not die in infancy. After all, they had not had opportunity to receive the revealing experience. Whatever the case, he could not bring himself to believe that his innocent children were suffering the torments of the eternally damned. It was unthinkable! During these confusing moments his faith in that particular harsh doctrine of his church yielded up its strength forever.

Upon arriving home John beheld the reality of the horrible tragedy. Sympathizing neighbors stood silently while others quietly gathered from the ashes what remained of the bodies of Eli and Elvira. Anne, sitting nearby on a log with little Zerelda Ann, caressed the infant to her bosom, while two-year-old Jennie sobbed at her side. At length, John and she walked alone into the woods to share their darkest hour.[13]

On a knoll just north of the Miller homestead, approximately one mile east and slightly north of the Plevna crossroads, is located the Miller graveyard. Because it is the only cemetery in the area dating from the time of John Smith's Hickory Flats' misfortune,[14] it is logical to conclude that it was there that the young couple placed what remained of the bodies of their two oldest children. Perhaps one or two of the many fieldstones which predate those with inscriptions were placed there by the grieving parents.

GRIEF UPON GRIEF

Sadly, this was not the end of the sorrow associated with Smith's Alabama venture. The shock from the loss of her children turned to abiding despair and Anne Smith could not escape its grasp. She was like the voice heard in Ramah, "Lamentation and bitter weeping; Rachel weeping for her children refused to be comforted...because they were not."[15]

The grieving mother soon sank into a deep depression and succumbed shortly thereafter.

Hickory Flats extends westward from the base of the Cumberland Plateau.

The Darkest Hour

As John departed the graveyard for the second time within a few weeks, he felt that he had been stripped of essentially everything he held most dear. Likewise, since the money from the sale of the farm had burned with the cabin, he was practically destitute of all earthly possessions. Remaining were his team and wagon which had brought him on his ill-fated journey, and with the exception of one, he could not locate the hogs and cattle he had driven from Kentucky.

Beyond these stunning misfortunes, and shortly after the burial of his wife beside the ashes of his children, John became gravely ill. He was stricken with what was diagnosed in his day as "the cold plague." From April until July his chances of survival seemed slight. However, with the patience and fortitude of Anna Miller, the daughter of a compassionate neighbor, he was eventually nursed back to health.

As soon as he could arrange to do so, with the assistance from considerate neighbors who aided in assembling the barest of necessities, he prepared to return to the friendly environs of the Little South Fork. One of his last gestures was to sell the lone surviving member of his fine herd of fifty cattle and present the proceeds to the doctor who had treated him during his close encounter with death. Leaving daughters Jennie and Zerelda in the care of friends, he turned northward and left behind a dream which had become an unbelievable nightmare.[16]

THE MILLER CEMETERY
The site of the Miller dwelling was beyond the cemetery. The graves of John Smith's wife and children would have been marked by field stones. Some stones with inscriptions date from near the time of Smith's Hickory Flats tragedy.

This cabin, believed to have been that of John and Anne Townsend Smith, has been restored and relocated in Monticello, Kentucky.

CHAPTER 7

A NEW BEGINNING
(1815-1817)

THE JOURNEY BACK

The mind of John Smith was a maze of complexities as he retraced his route northward through Tennessee toward the Little South Fork of the Cumberland River in southern Kentucky. A few months earlier he had traveled the same route with his devoted wife, four vibrant children, excellent herds of cattle and hogs, and enough money to purchase many acres. Less than one year later he traveled alone.

The contradictions into which John had been thrust pressed him to the fullest extent of human endurance. Instead of realizing a fortune from the Alabama soil, he had deposited within it the body of his beloved Anne and the ashes of their two oldest children. With friends back at Hickory Flats, Alabama, were three-year-old Jenny, the older of the two surviving children, and baby Zerelda Ann. As he traveled and reflected upon the fate of his innocent children, the doctrine of infant damnation became more and more inconsistent with what he knew of the Scriptures.

His first stop back in Kentucky was in Stockton's Valley where he visited with his seventy-four-year-old mother, who remained in the care of Jonathan, one of her younger sons. Friends in the Valley, some of whom had known the family for almost a score of years, wept with him as he recounted his sad experiences. He soon continued toward the region of the Little South Fork. Perhaps the greatest measure of relief he had experienced in months descended upon him as he rode into Parmleysville.

John proceeded directly to the home of William, his brother, whose wise counsel he highly valued. Once there he discovered that a letter from his old friend, Jeremiah Vardeman, was awaiting his return. Vardeman informed Smith that he knew of his misfortunes and related that a contribution had been made for his benefit by the churches of the Elkhorn Association.

The renowned preacher further advised John to attend the annual meeting of the Tates Creek Baptist Association which was in session during that current month. Vardeman instructed him that, in addition to receiving the contribution, he would have the good fortune of being in the presence of many well known preachers.[1]

RETURN TO CRAB ORCHARD

Smith set out immediately for Crab Orchard, the village in which he had first seen Jeremiah Vardeman twenty years earlier. The journey did not take long since he was well acquainted with the route.

The type of meeting at Crab Orchard to which Vardeman had invited John was a common occurrence on the Kentucky frontier. From very early in their history, Baptists made it a practice to group into associations their churches which were located within certain geographic boundaries. It was the practice of the associations to have one general meeting per year to which each church sent representatives or "messengers." After a moderator and clerk were chosen, any business which pertained to particular churches or to the association in general was transacted.

Accordingly, in August of 1815, the Tates Creek Baptist Association had convened for its annual session at Crab Orchard, Kentucky. At the appropriate time for the business portion of the association to be transacted, the melodious voice of Jacob Creath, Sr., one of the most respected Baptist preachers on the Kentucky frontier, called:

> Brother Moderator, it is impossible to transact the business of the Association in the midst of such a multitude as this. Many hundreds of people are yet without, and the house can hold no more. Let someone be appointed to preach to the people from the stand. This will engage the crowd, and we can go on with the business of the morning.[2]

It is not difficult to reconstruct the scene and climate of a gathering such as this. Large numbers generally attended these meetings. They usually lasted from Saturday through Monday, and it was not uncommon for members of entire families to be in attendance. For those who could not board in homes, camps were pitched in the area of the meeting.

A New Beginning

Horses were tied to trees and fence posts or grazed in the nearby fields. Wagons drawn to the meeting by the horses were depositories for the necessities required during these interesting and exciting times. Because these assemblies were of a social character as well as religious, had there been room in the meeting house for everyone, not all would have been interested enough in the affairs of the association to sit through the business sessions. Consequently, a crowd was usually milling around the site of the association meeting.

On this particular occasion, Thomas Hansford, the preacher at Crab Orchard, Kentucky, assisted with necessary arrangements. It will be remembered that it was by his preaching that the dance-loving Jeremiah Vardeman had been reclaimed to the Baptist fold approximately seventeen years earlier. Hansford began peering through the crowd in an attempt to find someone to preach to the large number of people who were in the vicinity of the building.

A familiar person dressed in a pair of homespun cotton pantaloons, loose, and far too short, arrested his attention. The object of Hansford's attention wore a cotton coat, once checked with blue and white but now of indistinguishable colors. On his head was a shapeless hat streaked with perspiration and dust, and over his shoes hung socks too large for his shrunken ankles.

The one upon whom Hansford's attention was focused was attired in a dirty, coarse shirt, unbuttoned at the neck. He wore no cravat (tie) because the only one he owned had been placed in the coffin of his wife whom he had buried approximately five months earlier. Hansford immediately recognized the man as John Smith.

"John!" called Hansford. "You must preach. The people will be glad to hear you."

Smith was first reluctant, perhaps sensitive about his appearance, but eventually mounted the stand which had been constructed in a nearby grove. Preceding Smith had been two young preachers who had attempted to speak but had failed because no miraculous message had come to them.

"If the Lord will not give it to me, brethren, then I cannot get it," remarked one of the two. The disappointed crowd began to disperse as Smith arose and timidly approached the speaker's stand.

Observing that some special means would be necessary to persuade the crowd to reassemble, Smith called, "Stay friends and hear what the great Augustine said!"

Detecting that he had begun to gain the attention of the crowd, he continued, "Augustine wished three things before he died. He wished to see Rome in her glory and purity, Paul on Mars' Hill, and Jesus in the flesh."

His novel approach elicited the attention of a few who chose to be seated. The majority smiled, however, and continued their departure.

"Will you not stay," Smith pled with increased volume, "and hear what the great Cato said?" Many returned, took their seats, and gave the appearance of those who anticipated being amused.

"Cato repented of three things before his death. First, he repented that he had ever spent an idle day; secondly, that he had ever gone on a voyage by water when he might have made the same journey by land; and thirdly, that he had ever told the secrets of his bosom to a woman."

Observing that the original crowd was now reassembling, to gain the attention of groups standing in the distance, with all the strength he could muster, he continued, "Come friends, and hear what the great Thales thanked the gods for."

With all seated and listening with much anticipation he related that "Thales thanked the gods for three things: first, that he was endowed with reason, and was not a brute; secondly, that he was a Greek, and not a Barbarian; and thirdly, that he was a man, and not a woman." [3]

The crowd became curious since quoting from the classics seemed very much out of character with the appearance of the speaker. The country preacher from Wayne County's Horse Hollow, whose formal education had been limited to approximately four months, had perhaps memorized the quotes from sources in the libraries of either Robert Ferrill or Rhodes Garth, his two most scholarly instructors.

Once the audience was settled, Smith observed:

> And now friends, I know you are ready to ask, 'And pray, sir, who are you?' I am John Smith, from Stockton's Valley. In more recent years, I have lived in Wayne, among the rocks and hills of the Cumberland. Down there, saltpeter caves abound, and raccoons make their homes. On that wild frontier we never had good schools, nor many books; consequently, I stand before you today a man without an education. But, my brethren, even in that ill-favored region, the Lord, in good time, found me. He showed me his wondrous grace, and called me to preach the everlasting gospel of his Son.[4]

A New Beginning

A MEMORABLE SERMON

With the undivided attention of the audience Smith read from Psalms 111:9: "He sent redemption to his people; he hath commanded his covenant forever; holy and reverend is his name." From the text he preached with fervor on "Redemption Conceived, Applied and Completed."[5]

It has been declared that Smith seemed inspired for the occasion and that:

> His voice like a trumpet reached and thrilled the most distant hearer, and his thoughts swept the audience like the storm sweeps the sea. The people crowded closer to hear him, and some who could find neither sitting nor standing room, climbed the trees, so that even the forest swayed to and fro as if under the magic spell in the third division, and portrayed the final glory of the redeemed. Every heart was filled with emotion, every eye was weeping, every face was radiant with hope, and at the close one loud "Amen" ascended to the heavens.[6]

Smith's remarkable presentation, in conjunction with his appearance that day on "the stand," and the declaration that he had lived among the raccoons and saltpeter caves on the rocky frontier, thrust him into an arena from which he would never withdraw.

Beginning on this occasion was a deep and lasting friendship with Jacob Creath, Sr., a mutual friend of Jeremiah Vardeman. The latter, for an unknown reason, had been prevented from attending the meeting of the association. However, indicative of Vardeman's genuine concern, he had arranged for the contribution of more than fifty dollars from the churches of the Elkhorn Association to be delivered by a representative.[7]

BACK ALONG THE LITTLE SOUTH FORK

Soon after the memorable Crab Orchard meeting John was overcome with a longing to see his children whom he had left with friends in Alabama. Making necessary preparations for the journey, he retraced the southern route that was by now quite familiar to him. In September the youthful father and his two young daughters departed Alabama in the same wagon which had transported them there approximately one year earlier. Jenny was three years old and Zerelda Ann was only fifteen months at the time of the lonely return to Kentucky.

Leaving the children in Stockton's Valley in the care of his aged mother and Jonathan, his brother, he continued his journey to the friendly environs of Parmleysville. Pleased to be back among people whom he had come to love, he resumed his preaching at Bethel Baptist Church, regretting that he had ever chosen to pursue an elusive dream. As he reflected upon the complexities attending his absence from the Little South Fork region, he did so with the feeling that God had chastised him for fostering secular motives which had sent him so far from where he needed to be.

Events moved swiftly during the two years between the fall of 1815 and the comparable season of 1817. By some means he managed to come into possession of a portion of "wild" land near his previous farm. Beyond attempting to reestablish himself in farming, Smith continued preaching along the Little South Fork with a measure of acceptability exceeding anything he had previously known.

During this period of time he was introduced to some literature which proved to be very timely in his transition from orthodox Calvinism. A preacher friend presented him a book by Andrew Fuller entitled *Gospel Worthy of All Acceptation*. Even though he was not prepared to completely accept Fuller's position, there was some consolation in the English author's idea of a general atonement.[8]

A NEW WIFE AND A NEW LOCATION

During the fall of 1815 John Smith became close to the Hurt family who resided in the Parmleysville neighborhood. He became especially fond of Nancy Hurt, who, in addition to sharing the industrious and frugal qualities of her family, was endowed with an extraordinary measure of kindness which appealed to the sensitivity of the young widower. Those professing an interest in the welfare of the young preacher who had known so much grief and deprivation would not have chosen Nancy as his mate because of her poverty. They would have much preferred for him the economic relief which would have resulted from his marrying into more comfortable circumstances.

Convinced that he had already been the object of divine chastisement for his materialistic ambitions, Smith never considered making a choice between Nancy's poverty and the possibility of wealth. Accordingly, he proposed to her and immediately departed for a tour into central Kentucky. At Nicholasville he further strengthened his recent acquaintance with Jacob Creath and at David's Fork, near Lexington, appreciated the companionship of Jeremiah Vardeman.[9]

A New Beginning

After the rewarding tour to the north Smith returned to Parmleysville on December 23, 1815. On December 25 the thirty-two-year-old widower married twenty-four-year-old Nancy Hurt.[10] His choice of her would prove to be one of the wisest decisions of his life.

In the process of recovering from the losses inflicted by the Alabama tragedy, John gained wider acceptance as an effective preacher. This success was complemented by his new wife who was totally committed to assisting in his aspirations. Only a geographic change remained for him to experience a new beginning.

Jeremiah Vardeman continued to be relentless in his attempts to persuade Smith to move from the Little South Fork region to an area where the scope of his influence would be more extensive. In May of 1817 he again visited central Kentucky and preached at Lulbegrud and Grassy Lick Baptist Churches in Montgomery County. Finally, with Nancy in full accord, Smith yielded to the wishes of Vardeman and consented to move to Montgomery County.[11]

The last entry in the October minutes of the Bethel Baptist Church of Christ at Parmleysville simply states: "Brother John Smith made application for a letter of dismission. It was granted."[12]

Nothing more is recorded of the departure. Having disposed of his small farm, livestock and crops, with household goods and family members in a wagon, the thirty-three-year-old preacher-farmer departed the region of the Little South Fork of the Cumberland on October 22, 1817.[13]

CHAPTER 8

JOHN SMITH'S DIFFICULT
FIELD OF LABOR
(1801-1818)

The Commonwealth of Kentucky was admitted to statehood in 1792, eleven days before Mount Sterling was given legal recognition by the legislature. Montgomery County, the eventual home of John Smith, was organized four years later and Mt. Sterling, formerly known as "Little Mountain Town," became the seat of government. The county was named in honor of General Richard Montgomery of Revolutionary War fame. The boundaries lay both east and west of the old Indian War Path.[1]

Located on the well traveled route used by Indians for hunting excursions or for traversing Kentucky from the Cumberland Gap to the Ohio River, the area was vulnerable to attack. However, as a result of the 1794 defeat of the Indians by General Anthony Wayne in the Battle of Fallen Timbers, the frontier became generally safer.[2] With the allaying of the Indian menace, preachers were permitted to enlarge their evangelistic circles with less fear of leaving their families unattended.

Baptist ministers in Montgomery County began meeting two pressing challenges. The first presented to the frontier preachers was that of gathering into congregations members who had become scattered along the frontier. A search of literature dealing with the activity of Baptist preachers in the central Kentucky area reveals that Moses Bledsoe, Robert Elkin, and David Barrow were especially busy in Clark and Montgomery Counties.

The Mt. Sterling Baptist Church was established in 1793 within the area which became Montgomery County.[3] Also organized during the same year were Lulbegrud and Grassy Lick Baptist Churches,[4] both located in the western half of the county. The Lulbegrud congregation soon constructed what was known as "the most appealing house of worship to be found on the frontier."[5]

Even though 1796 is the date most commonly given for the establishment of Spencer Creek Baptist Church, one credible source indicates that in 1795 the church was admitted as a new congregation into the South Kentucky Association of Separate Baptists.[6] Perhaps the organization of the Spencer Creek Church came somewhat later than the one in Mt. Sterling and those at Lulbegrud and Grassy Lick because of an uneasiness which lingered over the eastern end of the county. An Indian attack at Morgan's Station, located at the confluence of Spencer and Slate Creeks, had claimed the lives of nineteen women and children during 1793, the year during which the other Montgomery County churches were established.[7]

While these congregations were being organized, John Smith, the eventual preacher who would plead with them for a return to the New Testament order, was a lad of ten years and in the process of migrating from the Valley of the Holston in East Tennessee to southern Kentucky's Stockton's Valley.

NORTH DISTRICT ASSOCIATION OF UNITED BAPTISTS

The second challenge confronting Baptist preachers was that of organizing associations composed of churches within particular geographic areas. As was the case in the establishment of churches, Barrow and Bledsoe of Mt. Sterling and Elkin of Providence Baptist Church in Clark County led the way in assembling the framework of an organization which would accommodate the geographical and theological blend of the churches they served.

Overcoming the difficulties involved, the North District Association of United Baptists was formed in 1801. With Barrow serving as moderator and Elkin as "host pastor" at Providence, the Regular Baptists, who required strict adherence to the Philadelphia Confession of Faith, and the Separatist congregations, who rejected the confession as a creed, could both be admitted to membership in the association. Bledsoe assisted in authoring the "Terms of General Union" which permitted both groups to function within the same organizational framework.[8]

The success of those who effected the organizational union of the Regular and Separate Baptists was aided by the tide of religious fervor sweeping the frontier at the turn of the nineteenth century. Designated as the Second Great Awakening, the intensified interest in spiritual matters was conducive to camp meetings attracting huge crowds. The keen fervor which resulted in thousands "getting religion" reached an apparent climax in the memorable Bourbon County Cane Ridge Revival of 1801. Consequently, conditions prevailing at the time, rather than the skill of men, were given credit for the uniting of the two Baptist groups into one association because:

> What good and great men could not accomplish by argument, was at length brought about by the strange religious excitement, which in 1801, spread over the state, and destroyed the pride in doctrine, and the lust for priestly power in so many hearts.[9]

Included within the bounds of the North District Baptist Association were the counties of Clark and Montgomery. Cane Spring Baptist Church, situated immediately south of the Kentucky River in Madison County, was included because of its being contiguous to the churches in southern Clark County. When Bath County was carved from Montgomery in 1811, the boundaries of North District Baptist Association included three counties.

JOHN SMITH TO THE "DESTITUTE" CHURCHES OF MONTGOMERY

Following the organization of churches and the formation of associations the most difficult challenge for Baptist preachers was to keep the peace among those within their ranks who clung to various doctrinal positions. The religious fervor at the time did not continue long enough, nor did it run deeply enough, to prevent the diversity within Baptist groups from manifesting itself. An examination of issues resulting in dissension reveals why a peaceful union over an extended period of time was not possible.

The predestination and total depravity provisions of Calvinism were rejected by the Separatists but embraced by the Regular Baptists. With respect to the total depravity provision of the Philadelphia Confession of Faith, the moral condition of infants was a serious issue. Missions, as understood within the context of the time, were rejected by the Regulars but perpetuated by the Separatists. The latter rejected the notion of limited atonement and accepted Jesus as dying for everyone.

Within Montgomery County, Spencer Creek Baptist Church was distinctively Separatist while Lulbegrud was Regular Baptist and styled as "hyper-Calvinistic." The Baptist Church in Mt. Sterling, in stressing the strength of its Calvinistic persuasion, termed itself as Particular

Baptist. It was strongly anti-missionary in that it resisted any effort to preach to sinners, contending that Jesus did not need assistance from feeble humans to save anyone. Grassy Lick was recognized as being Calvinistic, but subsequent events suggest a segment somewhat susceptible to Separatist and "Reform" ideas.[10]

The unsettled religious climate was further compounded among all Baptist groups by the emancipation issue which centered around David Barrow. Barrow, minister of the church in Mt. Sterling, became obsessed with the evils of holding another human being in bondage. His abolitionist views spread to associations beyond North District and resulted in much dissension. It can be understood why such unrest was precipitated by the slavery issue when the census of 1810, for Mt. Sterling alone, indicates that of three hundred twenty-five people in the town, seventy-six, or twenty-three percent, were listed as slaves.[11]

Divided over slavery, missions, and the moral condition of infants, North District was an association in deep trouble. The fragile mooring of the district, at best an uneasy alliance between the various Baptist groups bound together by the "Terms of General Union" of 1801, was on the verge of disintegrating.

It was into this hotbed of contention that Jeremiah Vardeman persuaded thirty-three-year-old John Smith to come to Montgomery County in 1817. Styling the congregations as the "destitute" churches of Montgomery, Vardeman wrote to Smith, informing him that:

> He had withdrawn from the churches in Montgomery, but that the Lord had thereby opened a door of usefulness to him. The brethren there, he had not doubt, would be glad to have his services, and, he thought, they would liberally acknowledge them.[12]

In a letter, dated May 1, 1817, to James Mason of Grassy Lick in Montgomery County, Vardeman wrote:

> I have the pleasure to inform you that brother John Smith, from Wayne County, will be at Lulbegrud the third Saturday and Sunday in May, it being the time of their yearly meeting; and on the day following, will be at Grassy Lick. I think it would be to your spiritual interest to obtain his labors at Grassy Lick and the neighboring churches. I know not that he will move his residence; but it will not be amiss to try him. I am sorry that I am so circumstanced as not to be able to visit you more frequently. It has been a maxim with me to preach where the prospect of usefulness is the most flattering; and I am convinced that it is my duty to withdraw from Montgomery, at the present.[13]

It was soon evident that what had been disconcerting circumstances for Vardeman, after seven years of preaching in Montgomery County, proved to be a challenge to Smith. Whereas the problems of North District Baptist Association had subdued Vardeman, the country preacher from Horse Hollow conquered her and within a short time completely changed her composition.

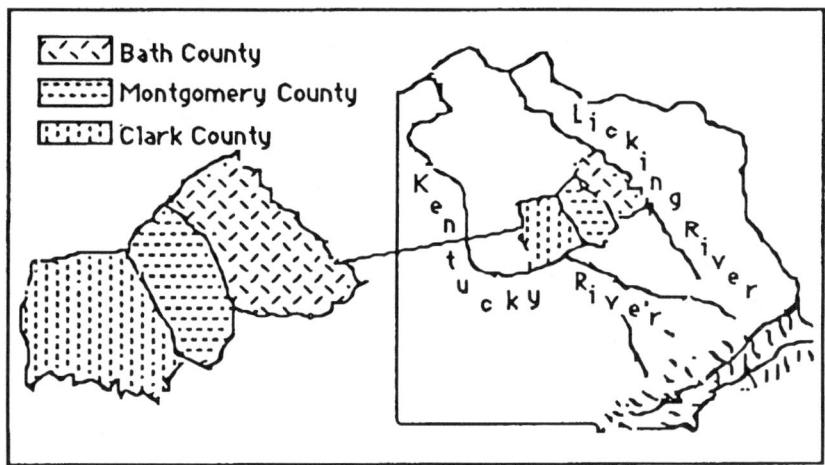

NORTH DISTRICT BAPTIST ASSOCIATION
North District Baptist Association was composed of Bath, Clark, and Montgomery Counties. Because of its proximity to the southern boundary of the district, Cane Spring, located immediately south of the Kentucky River in Madison County, was considered a part of the association.

CHAPTER 9

A VEXATIOUS INTRODUCTION
(1817-1822)

When John and Nancy Smith arrived in Montgomery County in late fall of 1817, their family consisted of three children. Jennie and Zerelda, the daughters who had survived the Alabama tragedy, were now five and three respectively. In May of that year Nancy had given birth to Eliza Blaze. The little girl, her first born, was named for Nancy's mother.[1]

The Smiths first moved to a rented farm in the Grassy Lick community. During the fall of 1818 a committee composed of members from the churches for which he preached chose for him a one-hundred-acre choice plot of land located two miles east of Mount Sterling. Arrangements were made for its purchase.

The first payment for the farm, which was valued at three thousand two hundred dollars, was to be made by the meager sum Smith had received from the sale of his Wayne County land. Subsequent payments arranged in a series of notes to come due at intervals were to be made by the four churches which he served.[2]

The location of Old Bethel, one of the churches to which Smith initially came, cannot be located with absolute certainty. Claims have been made that it was located in Clark County, but they lack validity. There was a Bethel community in Montgomery County, located in a portion which became the county of Bath in 1811, but evidence to support its being the Old Bethel of 1817 is lacking. Whatever the case, the congregation did not significantly enter into the shaping of early events in Smith's Montgomery County experiences.

John Smith's farm was located two miles east of Mt. Sterling on the south side of present-day Osborne Road. The late Stanley Kerns of Mt. Sterling assisted in verifying the location.

GRASSY LICK POTPOURRI

Even though the exact site of the original building has not been ascertained, the Grassy Lick of John Smith's day was located approximately five miles northwest of Mt. Sterling. The congregation had prospered for a time under the preaching of Jeremiah Vardeman but had entered a period of decline just previous to the withdrawal of his services. Upon moving to Montgomery County, John and Nancy Smith formally placed their membership with the Grassy Lick Church. Minutes of the North District Baptist Association reveal that for a decade Smith often served as one of her messengers to the annual meeting of the association.[3]

The church at Grassy Lick had the advantage of capable leadership to complement some of the most talented preachers in Kentucky who had come to serve her. In addition to Vardeman, her pulpit had been graced by Jacob Creath, Ambrose Dudley, and Moses Bledsoe. However, the various shades of doctrinal opinion, represented by the different preachers who had been to Grassy Lick, had resulted in persuasions among its members ranging from orthodox Calvinism to that of general atonement.[4]

A Vexatious Introduction

James Mason was among the outstanding leaders at Grassy Lick. As previously noted, Jeremiah Vardeman had corresponded with Mason in arranging for Smith to come to the church.

CONTENTIOUS LULBEGRUD

Lulbegrud, which received its strange name from a small stream in the area, was located three miles southwest of Mt. Sterling. It is believed that the strange name for the stream, and subsequently for the church, was assigned by a member of Daniel Boone's first excursion party into Kentucky. In their possession was a copy of Jonathan Swift's *Gulliver's Travels*, read during times of relaxation to relieve boredom and to stimulate meaningful conversation. "Lorbrulgrud" was among the words conjured up by the gifted satirist in attempts to convey to prudent people certain injustices which should be avoided.[5] Another source suggests that the name could possibly have been derived from a Shawnee Indian word meaning "bloody water."[6]

The nature of some of the events transpiring at Lulbegrud rivaled the strangeness of its name. Prior to Smith's arrival the congregation had divided over a log Jilson Payne had taken from the church property. Payne, needing a poplar log of a dimension conducive to the hewing of a salt box for curing meat, cut the tree from property he had contributed to the church. Subsequently, opposition to his action resulted in the church dividing. Almost two centuries later, perpetuating the folly of Lulbegrud, the salt box remains in the basement of the old house previously owned by Jilson Payne.[7]

Experiencing rather slow growth in the beginning, Lulbegrud Baptist Church grew rapidly for a time with the coming of Jeremiah Vardeman in 1810. However, by 1816, during the annual meeting of North District Baptist Association, the congregation was declared to be "in disorder." Ironically, Lulbegrud was serving as host church for the meeting during that time.

In 1817, the year Jeremiah Vardeman decided to sever his relations with Lulbegrud, the minutes of the annual meeting, unaltered from their original form, state:

> On motion, it was agreed to take up the business as arranged by the committee, and the case of Lulbegrud being the first, a question was taken—has that church acceded to the advice given her last Association? and decided in the affirmative. The Question was then taken—Is she now in order? and it was decided in the negative.[8]

It was evident that the association was becoming disgusted with contentious Lulbegrud. As would be suspected, by the time Vardeman departed the church was in a period of decline. After Smith began preaching for the strife ridden congregation, however, a period of revival followed which resulted in one hundred twenty-five additions to the church.[9]

The author is shown beside the infamous log "which split the church" at Lulbegrud.

For thirty years the most influential leader at Lulbegrud was James French. Following his training at prestigious William and Mary College in Williamsburg, Virginia, he began early to distinguish himself in a variety of areas. At the age of nineteen, when the American colonies rebelled against Great Britain, he volunteered for service in the cavalry. He and his younger brother were members of George Washington's tattered army which spent the dreadful winter of 1777-78 at Valley Forge.

Following the War for American Independence, French's interest turned to the District of Kentucky, Virginia's territory beyond the mountains to the west. He was appointed official surveyor of Madison County, Kentucky, by Governor Patrick Henry of Virginia. In June of 1783, in the fort at Boonesboro, he was married to Keziah Callaway, the youngest sister of the Callaway girls who were captured by the Indians during the early days of the outpost. French was

A Vexatious Introduction

twenty-seven years old at the time of the marriage while his young bride was only fourteen.[10]

James and Keziah French moved to Montgomery from Madison County in 1802 and became identified with the Lulbegrud Baptist Church. It is believed that Keziah was responsible for the planning of the impressive building which the Lulbegrud congregation constructed. J. H. Spencer, respected Baptist historian of the nineteenth century, stated: "Previous to 1810, this church exhibited a singular conceit in building a house of worship with twelve corners, to represent the twelve apostles." [11]

Soon after joining the Lulbegrud church James French began serving as clerk for both the church and for the North District Baptist Association of which Lulbegrud was a member. He and John Smith became acquainted when the latter became the preacher at Lulbegrud in 1817. The two entertained a mutual respect, but the "hyper-Calvinism" of French prevented them from becoming effective co-workers. Smith served Lulbegrud for five years, terminating his work there in 1823.[12]

SITE OF OLD LULBEGRUD BAPTIST CHURCH
The tombstone of Thomas Boone, great nephew of Daniel Boone, keeps a lonely vigil over the site of old Lulbegrud Baptist Church. The inscription states:
> He united to the church in 1800.
> He commenced preaching in 1812. Ordained in 1815.
> He had charge of the Lulbegrud church for about 40 years.
> "The Holy Spirit is a wind that brings dry bones to life and heals all diseases."

SEPARATIST SPENCER CREEK

In April of 1818 Smith began preaching at Spencer Creek Baptist Church, the antithesis of Lulbegrud. It was said of Spencer Creek:

> The members of the church were generally Separate Baptists; and though they had cordially entered the general union of 1801, they attached little importance to the five points of Calvinism or, in fact, to any other speculative system of belief.[13]

With this disposition it can be readily understood why the new preacher and the Spencer Creek Church formed a very close working relationship. None of the other churches served by Smith could identify with him so well during this period when his transition from the basic provisions of Calvinism was in process.

Unlike Smith's relationship with any of the other original churches for which he preached, that with Spencer Creek endured consistently to the end of his life. John Coons, clerk of the church for more than a half century, became an invaluable co-worker with Smith, as together they led the congregation into the flow of the movement to restore the order of the first century church. John and Nancy were close to the congregation not only in sentiment, but also geographically, since their farm was only about three miles from the Spencer Creek building.

CONTROVERSIAL MOUNT STERLING

Even though Smith did not begin preaching in Mt. Sterling until after the death of David Barrow in 1823, he was well acquainted with the town and the church. Barrow, the preacher in Mt. Sterling for a quarter of a century, was referred to as the "most distinguished" Baptist preacher among the emancipationists in Kentucky and without exception the ablest writer among them at the beginning of the nineteenth century. Because of his talent and education Barrow was at first widely known as the "wise man" before his strong stance against slavery essentially isolated him.[14]

Soon after Mt. Sterling became a member of the North District Baptist Association the district withdrew from Barrow because of his abolitionist activities among its churches. Rather than recognize the withdrawal of their preacher the Mt. Sterling Church withdrew from the association. Not until 1823, after the death of Barrow and the coming of John Smith as the preacher, did the church re-enter the North District.[15]

A Vexatious Introduction

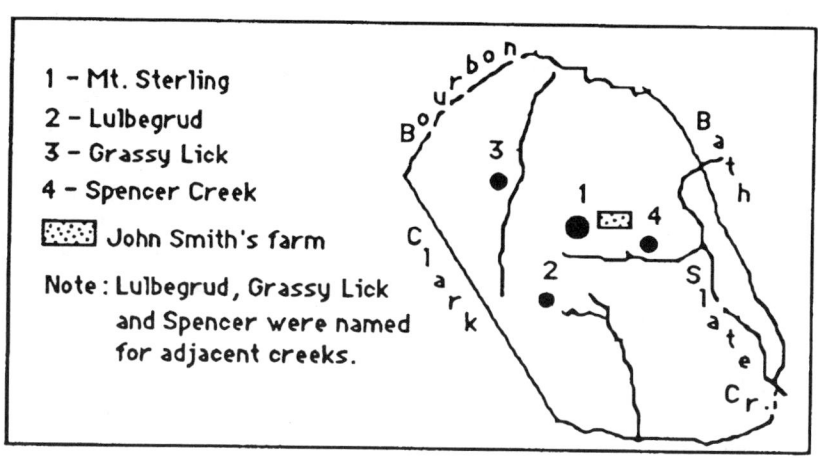

John Smith began preaching at Lulbegrud and Grassy Lick in 1817. Spencer Creek was added to his circuit in 1818. Smith succeeded David Barrow at Mt. Sterling in 1823, the year he ceased at Lulbegrud.

ECONOMIC HARDSHIPS

Following the War of 1812 Montgomery County fared rather well during the second decade of the nineteenth century. When John and Nancy Smith committed themselves to the purchase of their farm in 1818, the economic climate appeared to be favorable. Forces beyond Montgomery County, however, began to affect the local economy during the following year.

Poor management by the Second Bank of the United States during a time of overextension of credit and declination of European purchasing triggered the first serious financial panic in the history of the young republic. A depression, which followed the Panic of 1819, continued well into the 1820's. There were many bank foreclosures on mortgaged property and numerous state banks collapsed.[16]

Just as many other citizens of Montgomery County, the Smiths suffered greatly from declining prices and a decrease in the price of land, much of which had been purchased with borrowed money.[17] An unexpected turn of events compounded the economic problems for John and Nancy. The churches for which he preached failed to make the annual payments on his farm indebtedness as they had previously agreed to do.[18]

It is rather difficult to even remotely ascertain the reasons why the churches faltered on their commitments to assist their diligent preacher. The depression certainly would be understood to have been a factor, but regardless of the depressed economy there were families in all of the churches who were well established financially. Among them was James French of Lulbegrud, who not only owned much land but also served as a judge. Beyond doubt, he could have rendered assistance and lightened the burden of the dedicated preacher.

The Coons family at Spencer Creek, which also had access to excellent farm land, had been established in the area for a quarter of a century. The same was true of the Masons, Yeats, Gaitskills, and others at Grassy Lick. It appears that the burden, if mutually shared, would not have been great.

Although it is merely conjecture, there remains one possibility for the negligence among the churches. John Smith made no secret that certain doctrinal doubts perplexed him.[19] Therefore, any wavering on orthodox Calvinism would have been offensive to Lulbegrud and to many at Grassy Lick. The majority at Spencer Creek, being Separatist Baptist in persuasion, would not have been shaken by his doubts concerning election and predestination, but could have been somewhat disconcerted by not being exactly certain of his religious position at that particular time.

Smith struggled to pay the interest on his notes by working diligently on his land, but it soon became apparent that he would lose the farm unless someone assisted him in consolidating his several notes with a loan from the bank. At the point when he was most desperate, Colonel John Williams, an uncle of John Augustus Williams,[20] the 1870 biographer of Smith, assisted in making acceptable arrangements with the Commonwealth Bank of Mt. Sterling. His several notes were consolidated and the indebtedness was transferred to that institution.[21]

A HASTY ORIENTATION

Despite his financial difficulty and the fact that the churches paid him nothing for his labors, Smith continued to preach with fervor. The level of his profile among the churches in 1818, the first full year of his residence in Montgomery County, is unknown, since the minutes of North District Baptist Association do not exist for that year. A review of extant records, however, reveals that for the next decade he was exceedingly busy and figured prominently in the proceedings of the association.

A Vexatious Introduction

In 1819 Spencer Creek Baptist Church served as host church for the annual meeting of the association and Smith served as one of the messengers representing Grassy Lick. Before the meeting closed, he was chosen to preach the introductory sermon the following year. Accordingly, when the North District Association of Baptists met at Unity in Clark County during July of 1820, the minutes stated: "Introductory Sermon by Elder John Smith, from part of the 8th verse of third chapter of 1st Peter; 'Finally, be ye all of one mind.'"

The minutes further stated:

> The Moderator, Clerk, and brethren Jilson Payne, John Smith, and William Rash, jun. [sic] appointed to arrange the business of this Association, and report on Monday next.

The moderator was David Chenault of Cane Spring and the clerk was James French of Lulbegrud, two of the most seasoned Calvinists within the bounds of the association. Within that decade they both would become ardent adversaries of John Smith. However, this involvement reveals that Smith had quickly established himself among his associates within North District Baptist Association.[22]

At the same time that John was very busy with preaching and farming, his family was growing. In May of 1819 Nancy gave birth to Jonathan, her second child and first born son. However, joy was turned to grief the following month when little two-year-old Eliza Blaze died.[23]

The trials and tribulations experienced by John and Nancy Smith were typical of those suffered by many pioneer families. However, in the case of the Smiths, the distress during their early years in Montgomery County was compounded by their disappointment in the churches which they served. Had those congregations made the payments on the Smith farm, as they had committed themselves to do, their burden would have been somewhat lighter.

A FRUSTRATED SERMON

Financial struggles were not new for John Smith. He knew very well what it meant to eke a bare subsistence from the often harsh frontier. A beginning from possessing nothing, and a new beginning after losing everything, were akin to deprivation which had been much a part of his life. Because she had known poverty, Nancy qualified well as a companion to assist her husband during these difficult times.

Piercing religious conflicts, however, had elicited far more concern than had his financial struggles. Fifteen years earlier he had been wracked by anxieties related to his deep longing for an experience which would serve as evidence that he was among the elect of God. Likewise, probing his mind and monitoring his environment for a miraculous call to preach had resulted in nothing conclusive.

Compounding the discordant provisions of Calvinism was the loss a few years earlier of his two innocent children during the dreadful Alabama tragedy. With his Calvinistic tenets already under suspicion, that tragedy, with the possibility that his children were among the non-elect, had subjected him to certain rumblings that would not permit him to be at peace with himself. As he studied his Bible and continued to preach, he was pervaded by a restlessness which was the consequence of conflicts of both events and doctrine.

The nature of John Smith would not permit him to acquiesce when confronted with any matter which did not appear to be scriptural. Even though he was reluctant to fully subscribe to it, his recent introduction to the general atonement idea promulgated by Andrew Fuller assisted him in becoming more curious as to whether or not basic doctrines which he had been taught, and had himself taught, could be supported by Scripture. As he pondered apparent conflicts, he was being led closer to the total abandonment of Calvinism.

Preaching at Spencer Creek in March of 1822, the divergent courses of Calvinistic doctrine and the Scripture led him into an inescapable dilemma. With zeal he exhorted sinners to hear and believe the gospel. In urging them to repent and submit to the Savior, he informed them: "Jesus died for you, but if you believe not, you must be damned."

As never before, he immediately perceived an obvious conflict. According to Calvinism, there were no means by which the elect could be lost and the non-elect saved. Therefore, he reasoned, if the non-elect should believe, their faith would be in vain. On the other hand, should the elect not believe, it still would make no difference in their eternal destiny. He could no longer accept the notion of the elect being saved, even if they denied the truth, and the non-elect being lost even though they believed it. The direction in which logic was taking him would not permit the honest, conscientious preacher to continue exhorting the audience.

At length he apologetically remarked, "Brethren, something is wrong—I am in the dark—we are all in the dark; but how to lead you to the light, or to find the way myself, I know not."[24]

In his frustration he moved from the pulpit to the pew. Once at home with Nancy he shared with her his confused thoughts, as was consistent with his practice. After they fervently prayed together for divine light, he pledged himself, both to heaven and to his wife, that he would take God's Word as his only oracle, examine it carefully, and calling no man master, follow its directions wherever they might lead him.[25]

At this juncture it is well to ponder the dedication of John and Nancy Smith. He was a relatively young man of thirty-four years and she a youthful twenty-five when they accepted the difficult Montgomery County assignment. Therefore, at best, their introduction to Montgomery County had been a vexatious one. His determination to continue preaching for churches who gave him no support, and her willingness to work the farm and care for the children while he was away, testified of their love for the Lord and for one another.

Better times eventually came, but not until after a decade of intense financial struggles.

CHAPTER 10

THE MERGING OF A MAN
AND A MOVEMENT
(1798-1822)

THE SECOND GREAT AWAKENING

Previous reference has been made to John Smith's 1799 encounter with one of James McGready's revivals. He had observed the responses of hundreds being "struck with an awful sense of their lost estate," and falling to the ground "as though slain" with "screams of mercy piercing the heavens." At times the cries of the distressed were almost as loud as the pleading of the preacher.[1] John was totally unimpressed and quite perplexed by what he had observed.

McGready, a fearless Presbyterian preacher, was one of the best known among zealous evangelists who introduced revivals to the Kentucky frontier at the dawning of the nineteenth century.[2] The religious fervor manifested in such revivals is designated by historians as the Second Great Awakening. It followed a time of religious indifference which generally characterized the era immediately following the Revolutionary War.

Deism, a system of thought based upon reason rather than divine revelation, had become popular among intellectuals. Materialism, a natural companion of deism, had permeated much of society. Accompanying the coldness in religion and pervading the frontier was an alarming measure of wickedness. In the clamor to move west and claim its potential treasures, little thought was given to matters of a spiritual nature. The minority who was sensitive to the quality of life had become deeply concerned.

The Second Great Awakening was especially a reaction to this period of religious indifference and widespread wickedness. Breaking out sporadically in many sections, the revivals were as emotionally charged as those of the earlier awakening which had brought to prominence preachers such as George Whitefield and Jonathan Edwards. In attempting to describe the spontaneity of the religious climate which began to express itself in revivals, one source made reference to "Kentucky Ablaze," and observed:

> Against the backdrop of recent deism, materialism, and widespread indifference in religion, these gigantic revival meetings with thousands in attendance, multitudes falling to the ground wailing and shouting, and reports of the miraculous transformations of entire communities, seemed all the more stupendous.[3]

Regular Baptists, the designation by which orthodox Calvinistic Baptists were generally known, resisted the extreme emotionalism associated with the revivals of the Second Great Awakening.[4] Therefore, the religious fervor of the time did little more than touch John Smith's Stockton's Valley and Isaac Denton's Clear Fork Baptist Church. With his religious orientation, it is understandable why John was unable to identify with such a phenomena as a mass frontier revival.

BARTON WARREN STONE AND THE GREAT REVIVAL

Barton Warren Stone, who was preaching in neighboring Bourbon county at the time John Smith moved to Montgomery, had visited one of McGready's Logan County meetings. Stone, the minister at Cane Ridge Presbyterian Church, returned home with the hope that a similar revival would spontaneously ignite within the parameters of his ministerial charge. His aspirations were realized when, in August of 1801, the religious fervor of the Kentucky frontier reached a crescendo in a memorable revival at Cane Ridge.[5]

The revivalistic spirit which prevailed affected Montgomery County in two ways. First, a climate was created in 1801, to which reference has previously been made, in which the Regular and Separatist Baptists were brought together within the organizational framework of the North District Association of United Baptists. Second, a revival estimated to have been attended by three thousand people occurred at Springfield Presbyterian Church, located approximately seven miles northeast of Mt. Sterling.

Barton Stone came from Cane Ridge to Springfield, which was located ten miles farther east, to assist Joseph Price Howe during the revival. For more than thirty years Howe was one of the most influential Presbyterian preachers on the Kentucky frontier. An account of the meeting suggests not only the import of the religious fervor which permeated the scene, but also alludes to the excesses and abuses which accompanied the revival phenomenon. It stated:

> At Springfield Mr. Howe had no other assistance but Mr. Stone [Rev. Barton W.]. The people were not so numerous as in Paris. Numbers fell down. One deaf and dumb person was affected in this way and signed afterwards that her distress was removed by a power from above. A number of people fell in distress. An old Baptist woman sold whiskey there and produced confusion as she had done at Paris. The number that attended were about 3,000.[6]

A RECALCITRANT BARTON STONE

While Joseph Price Howe remained with the Presbyterian Church until his death in 1826, subsequent events were different for Barton Stone, who, according to colleague David Purviance, "possessed an independence of mind and a freedom of thought which could not be bound."[7] Such a temperament would not permit him to succumb to the constraints imposed by the Westminster Confession of Faith, the creed of the Presbyterians.

The young "New Light" Presbyterian preacher had come as supply minister to Cane Ridge in Bourbon County in 1796. He also served the Concord Presbyterian Church in neighboring Nicholas County. After his ordination by the Transylvania Presbytery in 1798, Cane Ridge and Concord became his official charges. His response at the time of his ordination revealed a disposition consistent with the restoration spirit.

"Do you receive and adopt the Confession of Faith as containing the system of doctrine taught in the Bible?" Stone was asked at the time of his ordination.

"I do, so far as I see it consistent with the Word of God," replied the recalcitrant twenty-six-year-old preacher.[8]

Stone's continued resistance to the tyranny of the Westminster Confession of Faith led him, along with four other ministers, to make a complete break with the Presbyterians in 1803. They eventually took the designation of "Christian" for individual members of Christ's body and considered themselves to be members of the Church of Christ, free of all human labels.

Despite their pledge to adhere to biblical names, Stone and his colleagues proceeded to organize the Springfield Presbytery. However, in 1804 they became convinced that the organization was unscriptural. This conviction resulted in the penning of the classic "Last Will and Testament of the Springfield Presbytery." In part it stated:

> We will, that this body die, be dissolved, and sink into union with the Body of Christ at large: for there is but one body, and one Spirit, even as we are called in one hope of our calling.
>
> We will, that our name of distinction, with its Rever'd title, be forgotten, that there be but one Lord over God's heritage, and his name one.
>
> We will, that our power of making laws for the government of the Church, and executing them by delegated authority, forever cease; that the people may have free course to the Bible, and adopt the law of the Spirit of life in Christ Jesus.[9]

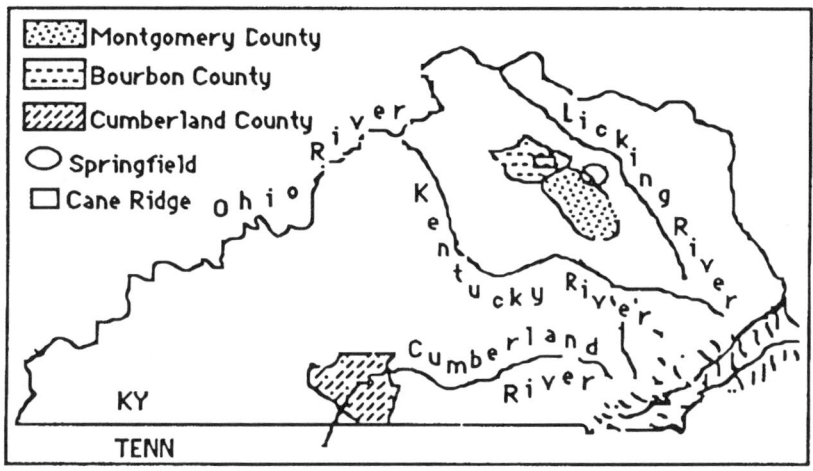

Following the Cane Ridge Revival, Barton Stone came to Springfield to assist Joseph Price Howe in a revival at which the attendance numbered an estimated three thousand. Stone was influenced by Rice Haggard's "Christians simply" position. Haggard's work was primarily in the Cumberland County area. The name of Springfield Presbyterian Church is not to be confused with that of the Springfield Presbytery.

CANE RIDGE MEETINGHOUSE
Constructed in 1791, the Cane Ridge building in now enclosed and preserved by a large stone structure.

RICE HAGGARD AND "CHRISTIANS SIMPLY"

In the wake of the American Revolution the quest for complete religious freedom prevailed among the Methodists as well as the Baptists and Presbyterians. Its results were eventually manifested on the Kentucky frontier. James O'Kelly and Rice Haggard rebelled against the autocratic aspirations of Francis Asbury, who desired to be head of the Methodist Episcopal Church in America. They designated their group as the Republican Methodist Church.[10]

The course pursued by O'Kelly and Haggard led them to lay aside human devices and to adopt the Bible alone as their rule of faith and practice. With that resolve, in 1794 Rice Haggard stood before the Lebanon Church in Surry County, Virginia, and made his memorable declaration that followers of Jesus should be known simply as "Christians." Later referring to that occasion, he remembered that, with Bible in hand, his words were:

Brethren, this is a sufficient rule of faith and practice. By it we are told that the disciples were called Christians, and I moved that henceforth and forever the followers of Christ be known as Christians simply.[11]

In 1807, the year during which Haggard located permanently in Cumberland County, near Burkesville, Kentucky, twenty-three-year-old John Smith was leading "social" meetings in homes in Horse Hollow. Even though they were geographically close, there is no evidence that Smith ever met Haggard, and it was many years before he manifested any interest in meeting Stone. At the time that these men were interested in restoring the ancient order, Smith was seeking a religious experience and a miraculous call to preach.

By way of qualification, while Haggard is given credit for bringing the designation of "Christian" to be accepted and widely applied by those interested in the restoration of the New Testament order, it is believed by researchers that he had been influenced by the pen of Benjamin Grosvenor. With Acts 11:26 as his text, Grosvenor, in London, England, had published a pamphlet entitled: "An Essay on the Christian Name; Its Origin, Import, Obligation, and Preference to All Party Denominations." Grosvenor, in turn, acknowledged that he had been influenced by other sources.[12]

Haggard is believed to have authored a pamphlet entitled, "An Address to the Different Religious Societies, on the Sacred Import of the Christian Name." Introducing the treatise, he wrote:

> Some may, perhaps be anxious to know who the author of the following pages is, his name, and to what denomination he belongs. Let it suffice to say, that he considers himself connected with no party, nor wishes to be known by the name of any—he feels himself united to that one body of which Christ is the head, and all his people fellow members.[13]

Haggard's resolve carried him much further than O'Kelly along the route toward total liberation from sectarianism. After coming to Kentucky his insistence upon employing the name "Christian" as the only designation for the saved influenced Barton W. Stone. Likewise, the pamphlet written by Haggard, which dealt with that revered name, is believed to have influenced the wording of "The Last Will and Testament of the Springfield Presbytery."[14]

The log house of Rice Haggard has been restored and relocated in Burksville, Kentucky.

ALEXANDER CAMPBELL—LATE COMER

Thomas Campbell came from Ireland to Washington, Pennsylvania, in 1807 and began preaching within the bounds of the Chartiers Presbytery. Soon at odds with both the presbytery and synod he departed the Presbyterians and with a small group of supporters established the Christian Association of Washington. Campbell was commissioned by the group to prepare an official statement of their position and intent. The resulting document was the scholarly and provocative "Declaration and Address." The challenge presented within its context to "Speak where the Bible speaks and to be silent where the Bible is silent" became the motto of the Restoration Movement.[15]

Alexander Campbell, the brilliant son of Thomas, followed his father to America, arriving during the year the elder Campbell penned the "Declaration and Address." When the document was presented to the son for his reaction, the latter was so impressed that he declared his intention to preach its sentiments over the span of his entire lifetime.[16] That commitment remained firm until his death in 1866, fifty-seven years after his noble affirmation.

Alexander's fame and brilliance exceeded that of the scholarly Thomas. It was his idea, rather than that of his father, that instead of supporting the sprinkling of infants the Scriptures taught that penitent believers should be immersed for the remission of sins. Accordingly, on June 12, 1812, Thomas and Alexander, their wives, Alexander's sister, and a Mr. and Mrs. James Hensen were baptized upon a confession of faith in Jesus Christ.[17]

The younger Campbell's distinction as a preacher and writer spread rapidly. His fame, especially among the Baptists, was enhanced following debates on the subject of baptism in 1821 and 1823. In the latter year he began publishing the *Christian Baptist* from his home in Bethany, Virginia.[18] The newly published journal became the medium of contact for John Smith with Alexander Campbell.

INDEPENDENT MOVEMENTS

When Thomas Campbell penned the "Declaration and Address," he had no knowledge of the efforts of Rice Haggard and Barton Stone. They, in essence, were attempting to produce on the Kentucky frontier that which Campbell envisioned in his famous document. Furthermore, though the precise date that Alexander Campbell and Barton Stone first came to know of one another is uncertain, it is known that they did not meet before the year 1824.[19]

As he struggled with the confusing issues during the early 1820's, John Smith of Montgomery no doubt knew about the "Stoneites" in neighboring Bourbon County. However, the disdain on the part of the Montgomery County Baptists for the Bourbon County "Christians" was somewhat akin to that of the Jews toward the Samaritans of old. Smith had no interest in meeting Stone.[20]

Just as Campbell and Stone had arrived at their respective positions independently of one another, John Smith had just as singularly come to his decisive point in 1822 with his "frustrated sermon" experience at Spencer Creek. At that juncture, when he committed himself to seek Bible solutions on doctrinal matters, he knew nothing of the positions of either Stone or Campbell. His aspirations, however, were just as noble as theirs.

CHAPTER 11

THE DECISIVE YEARS
(1822-1826)

A BUSY BIENNIUM

When John Smith stepped from the pulpit at Spencer Creek on that memorable Sunday in March of 1822, he was determined to follow the Scriptures wherever they led him. There was no way he could accurately envision the consequences of that affirmation. As he persisted in his revised course, he knew without a doubt that eventually there would be opposition from his North District colleagues. Even though he had shared some of his persisting frustrations concerning the provisions of Calvinism, he was fully accepted at the association meeting on the fourth Saturday in July of that same year.

Serving as moderator and clerk for the 1822 annual meeting were David Chenault of the Cane Spring Church and James French of Lulbegrud, two seasoned old Calvinists who would never be shaken from their revered moorings. The association was honored to have as its visitors Jeremiah Vardeman and Jacob Creath, Sr. of the Elkhorn Association. Vardeman and Creath, along with John Taylor of the Franklin Association and Walter Warder of the Bracken Association, were all appointed to preach the following day.

John Smith was very busy during the proceedings. In addition to serving as a messenger from the Grassy Lick Church, he was chosen to deliver letters to the corresponding associations of Elkhorn and Bracken, which were to be read at their next annual meetings. More importantly, he was selected to deliver the introductory address when the North District Baptist Association convened the following year.[1]

Several factors contributed to making 1823 a year of great significance in the religious transition of John Smith. First, after the

The Decisive Years

death of David Barrow, Smith terminated his work at Lulbegrud and began preaching for the Mount Sterling Baptist Church. He was succeeded at "hyper-Calvinistic" Lulbegrud by Thomas Boone,[2] a great nephew of Daniel. Thomas conformed precisely to the cadences of James French.

Second, with the preaching of the introductory sermon he became well established in the proceedings of the North District Baptist Association. The recorded minutes of the session at Log Lick in Clark County begin with: "Introductory sermon by Elder John Smith, from the 17th verse of the 5th Chapter, 2nd Corinthians—'Therefore, if any man be in Christ, he is a new creature; old things are passed away; behold, all things are become new.'" [3]

Perhaps the most significant of the events which transpired during the year was the introduction of the *Christian Baptist* to John Smith by Buckner Payne, a Mt. Sterling merchant.[4] Coming at an opportune time, following his "I'm in the dark" admission at Spencer Creek the previous year, the paper provided some much needed direction during a critical period. In the prospectus he read:

> The *Christian Baptist* shall espouse the cause of no religious sect, excepting that ancient sect called 'CHRISTIANS FIRST AT ANTIOCH.' Its sole object shall be the eviction of truth, and the exposure of error in doctrine and practice. The editor, acknowledging no standard of religious faith or works, other than the Old and New Testaments, and the latter as the only standard of the religion of Jesus Christ, will, intentionally at least, oppose nothing which it contains, and recommend nothing which it does not enjoin.[5]

When the North District Baptist Association met at Grassy Lick in July of 1824 John Smith was apparently satisfied to be selected moderator for the three-day session, regardless of the misgivings permeating his analytical mind. James French again was chosen as clerk and Jeremiah Vardeman, Smith's reliable old friend, preached on Sunday.[6] Paradoxically, at the same time that Smith's course away from the Baptists was taking a more certain direction, he was becoming more established within the association.

1824—THE COUNTRY PREACHER MEETS THE BETHANY SCHOLAR

Sometime during 1824 Smith learned that Alexander Campbell was scheduled to be in Flemingsburg, Kentucky, before proceeding to Mt.

Sterling. With a driving curiosity to meet a highly educated man who claimed to be a Christian but belonged to no religious party, Smith rode the thirty miles to Flemingsburg to meet Campbell. William Vaughn, a preacher of the Bracken Association, escorted him to the house where Campbell was lodging.

"Brother Campbell," said Vaughn, "I wish to introduce Brother Smith."

"Ah," replied Campbell, "and this is Brother Smith? I know Brother Smith very well, though I have never seen him before."

Having perceived that Kentucky was a potentially receptive field for the propagation of his restoration ideas, Campbell would certainly have encountered Smith's name as he monitored the area. Perhaps, too, he had heard something about Smith from Jeremiah Vardeman, whom Campbell had chosen the previous year to serve as moderator in his debate with W. L. McCalla at Washington, Kentucky. Whatever the case, a mutual respect began which endured until the death of Campbell forty-two years later.

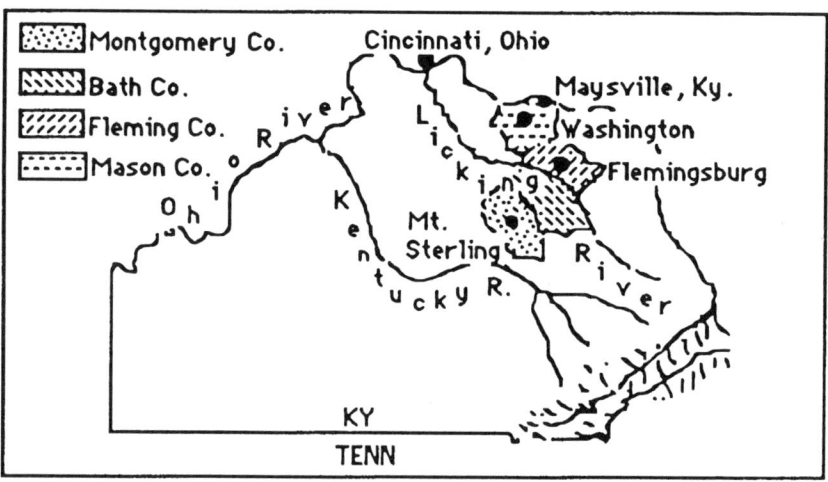

In 1824 John Smith traveled by horseback the distance of thirty miles from Mt. Sterling to Flemingsburg to meet Alexander Campbell. Campbell was familiar with that area of Kentucky since he had debated W.L. McCalla at nearby Washington the previous year.

At the appointed time for Campbell to speak, Smith took his seat on the floor of the platform near the feet of the renowned scholar. He intended to absorb every word emitted from the lips of the editor who had so completely captured his interest and curiosity. After presenting a general outline of the epistle to the Galatians the speaker focused on the allegory of Hagar and Sarah.

Following the sermon Smith remarked to Vaughn, "Brother Billy, is it not hard to ride thirty miles, as I have done, just to hear a man preach thirty minutes?"

"You are mistaken, Brother John. Look at your watch. It has surely been longer than that," answered Vaughn.

Discovering that Campbell had preached for two and one-half hours, Smith observed, "I have never been more deceived. Two hours of my life are gone; I know not how, though wide awake, too, all the time."[7]

After Campbell had spoken three times at Mt. Sterling, Smith continued with him toward Bourbon County. At North Middletown, located a short distance beyond the Montgomery County boundary, Smith turned back to Mt. Sterling while Campbell proceeded on to Georgetown for his first meeting with Barton Stone.[8] Smith's meeting with Stone would wait for another time.

1825—THE CONVERSION OF JACOB AND MATILDA JANE COONS

During 1825, approximately one year after John Smith met Alexander Campbell, his slowly forming perception of undenominational Christianity was further enhanced by another experience at Spencer Creek. It first centered around the desire of Jacob Coons, and eventually that of his wife, to become Christians according to the order of the New Testament.

Very little is known of Jacob Coons until he married the daughter of Joseph Price Howe, minister of the Mt. Sterling and Springfield Presbyterian Churches. As previously related, Howe was a colleague of Barton Warren Stone before the latter departed the Presbyterians.[9] While the marriage of Jacob and Matilda Jane precipitated an overt conflict between the Coons and Howe families, it brought the Presbyterian minister and John Smith of Spencer Creek Baptist Church into covert conflict. For approximately five years the young couple was very much the center of attention in both congregations.

The renowned Springfield preacher had been deeply troubled by his wayward daughter. Matilda Jane had rebelled against parental authority and had become "a thoughtless, worldly-minded woman" who acknowledged that she was "a vain and giddy creature and a great sinner."[10] One can imagine the anguish of the devoted Joseph Price Howe in his dealing with a brazen daughter who flaunted the principles of her respected family and the tenets of the Presbyterian Church.

Existing records reveal that when Matilda Jane and Jacob were married on November 8, 1820, the officiating minister was none other than Joseph Price Howe.[11] Marrying his wayward daughter to a Baptist boy was an agonizing experience for the respected Presbyterian preacher. Most assuredly Smith had a keen interest in the proceedings, since the Coons family was one of the strongest in the Spencer Creek Baptist Church.

Soon after his marriage to Matilda Jane, Jacob Coons presented himself before the church for immersion. Smith invited the respondent to impart to the assembly whatever he chose. The experience which Coons related was quite different from any that had been previously heard.

Standing before the assembled group, Jacob stated that he had "neither seen any strange sights, nor had he heard any strange sounds, but believing with all his heart that Jesus was the Christ, he wished to obey him."

Following Coons' statement, Smith arose and said, "Brethren, with the Bible in my hand, if I were to die for it, I do not know what other question to ask him!"

Occurring in October of 1825, the conversion of Jacob Coons is declared to be the first one on record among Baptists in Kentucky in which the relating of an experience before immersion was considered unnecessary. Concerning this case of one being baptized upon a simple confession of faith in Jesus Christ, it is stated:

> This incident, taking place with the approbation of a church that had no constitution or creed but the inspired Word, may be recorded as the first exemplification of the Ancient Order within the District, if not of the State.[12]

Jacob's immersion displeased Matilda Jane's family. Her father, attempting to confirm her in her early religious beliefs, gave her a tract entitled "Infant Church Membership" and encouraged her to share it with her husband. She studied the tract with Jacob as she had been instructed. He became very concerned when his wife emphatically declared of the tract that "It was God's truth."

The Decisive Years

In his perplexity, Jacob Coons turned to John Smith for assistance with his domestic problem. Smith instructed young Coons to have her ask of her father whether or not she was in the church. Jane did as she was instructed. Following is the essence of the conversation.

"Father," asked Jane, "Am I a member of the church?"

"Yes, my daughter, I initiated you when you were an infant."

"But father," the daughter inquired, "you know that I have always been a worldly-minded girl. Do you think that it is right for me to say that I am in the church?"

"Daughter," he replied, "You remember that, in the church, there are both tares and wheat; so the Savior teaches in the parable. You are but a tare, Jane! You are but a tare, I fear!"

Jane was satisfied, but Jacob was not. He turned to his preacher for further assistance. Following John Smith's advice, he returned home and initiated further conversation with Jane.

"Jane," inquired he, "didn't your father say that he had put you in the church when you were a child?"

"Yes, but he said that I was only a tare," replied his wife.

"Your father surely could not have put you in there, Jane; for the Book says, he that sows the tares is the devil!"

With this shocking revelation Jane was prompted to go again to her father to have this startling difficulty solved. Hopefully, he could lead her from the jaws of this harsh dilemma.

"Father," asked she, "Did you not tell me that you had initiated me into the church yourself?"

"Yes, my daughter; but what is it that bothers you now?"

With her Bible open and pointing to Matthew 13:39, she exclaimed, "Why father, look! He that sows the tares is the devil!"

Jane related that after her father looked at the passage of scripture she had presented, he groaned aloud and walked the floor but made no reply. Subsequently, her regard for the Scriptures increased, and with Smith instructing young Coons in how to deal with his wife and her father, Jane soon submitted to being baptized in the same manner and for the same purpose as her husband.[13]

Jacob and Matilda Jane became an unusually committed couple. He began preaching soon after his conversion and Jane remained an unwavering companion in his efforts for more than forty years. The conversion of the couple made an impact upon the Spencer Creek congregation and certainly upon John Smith during a critical stage in his transitional period.

The author studies the inscription on the grave of Joseph Price Howe located on the grounds of the Springfield Presbyterian Church. The renowned Springfield preacher died in 1826.

A CHANGING CLIMATE

In 1825, the year the North District Baptist Association met at Sycamore in Montgomery County, John Smith was again chosen as moderator and James French as clerk. Cane Spring's David Chenault preached the introductory sermon. Ironically, the further Smith grew away from the staunch Calvinistic position of French and Chenault, the closer he was placed with them in the proceedings of the annual meetings of the association.

The frequent choice of Smith, either as moderator or for the introductory sermon, was indicative of the favor he had gained among the messengers who represented the various churches composing the association. Among the messengers, however, were two exceptions. James French, though apparently kind to Smith, viewed him with suspicion. French perennially served as clerk because he was judged to be a capable writer and a meticulous record keeper. Likewise, David Chenault, who, with French, constituted an unofficial alliance in the defense of Calvinistic doctrine, was somewhat subdued in his relationship with the talented preacher whose star was rising among his colleagues.

There is an indication during this time that the perceptive French began sensing a changing climate within the association. In the circular letter to the churches during 1825 he chose to dwell upon the pain which had been inflicted by divisions which had occurred among the Baptists since their migration to the Kentucky frontier. He wrote:

> Thus the Baptists in this State, who a little upwards of forty years ago, consisted of but two sorts, regulars, and separates; differing nothing in externals, are now become six kinds of Baptists. And all these differ in sorts, (Universalists, and friends of humanity excepted) pretty numerous, supplied with preachers and bidding fair to extend and increase in numbers. And intermixed more or less with the united Baptists, which is the main body, and more numerous than all the others together. Of whom the Churches composing this association are part. And the united Baptists are not uniform in their conduct towards those other sorts of Baptists; for some of their associations are in correspondence with some of those other sorts of Baptists: while some other of their associations, withhold their correspondence from them all, and correspond with the united Baptists only. What is to be the end of these things, will not this contrariety, this inconstancy of the united Baptists in their correspondence, if persisted in, prove a root of bitterness, whereby many, if not all of them will be defiled? [14]

French was concerned that an already confused and unhappy situation was going to be compounded by additional strife and further division. Subsequent events revealed that his apprehension was justified.

1826—AN UNMISTAKABLE STAND

Perhaps to John Smith, Solomon's declaration that "there is a friend that sticketh closer than a brother" was best epitomized in the relationship between him and John Coons. From the inception of Smith's service in Montgomery, Coons had consistently served as a messenger for the Spencer Creek Baptist Church. Under their combined leadership Spencer had grown from thirty members in 1817 to one hundred fifty-three in 1826.[15]

Born in Culpepper County, Virginia, John Coons, the older brother of Jacob, had come to the Spencer Creek section in 1794, two years before the organization of Montgomery County. In the year of

1792 he had received a letter from a relative which included an invitation to come to Kentucky, inasmuch as a bride had been chosen for him "out here in the West." The inducement was sufficient to lure the nineteen-year-old John Coons through Cumberland Gap and along the hazardous Wilderness Road to Bryan's Station, a frontier settlement located near Lexington.

The adventure culminated in his marriage to Elizabeth Ellis, the daughter of Captain William Ellis, who had come to Kentucky in 1781 from Spotsylvania County, Virginia. Captain Ellis had served as the military attache for Lewis Craig's Traveling Church. Immediately after their marriage John and Elizabeth moved thirty-five miles east of Lexington to make their home on land she had received by the bequest of her father.[16]

When Spencer Creek Baptist Church in Montgomery County was organized in 1795, John and Elizabeth Ellis Coons were among the first members. After John Smith began preaching at Spencer Creek, he and John Coons became inseparable co-workers. During the 1820's they moved together from the Baptist persuasion to that of Alexander Campbell's reformers. Two years after Campbell had visited Montgomery County in 1824, Smith and Coons made public their position and included it in the records of the Spencer Creek Church. In part it stated:

> We therefore, for the information of those who may live after we are gone; we think proper to say that now in the year of our Lord 1826 we do believe that the word of God is the only rule of faith and practice, and that the Church of Jesus Christ according to the New Testament is composed of members who have been baptized by immersion in water upon the profession of their faith in Jesus Christ and that no other mode on subjects are [sic] authorized by the word of God...therefore, disclaiming all human authority as the standard or rule of faith and manners, we do agree as a church to maintain the worship of God according to the New Testament....
>
> Signed: John Smith, Minister
> John Coons, Clerk [17]

The sentiment expressed in the above statement, following the memorable conversion of Jacob Coons the previous year, indicates that Spencer Creek was on its way out of the Baptist fold.

When the association met at Mt. Sterling in July of 1826, Smith, perhaps busy with details involved in hosting the annual meeting, did not figure prominently in the proceedings. However, indicative of his growing influence was his selection to serve as an alternate to Thomas Boone in delivering the introductory sermon at Cane Spring the following year.[18]

The years of 1822-26 had been decisive ones. During 1822-23 Smith had become well established among his colleagues of the North District Baptist Association. Into his hands had come the *Christian Baptist*, which had proved invaluable in charting his revised course.

He had met Alexander Campbell in 1824 and was much impressed with the scholarship of the *Christian Baptist* editor. The conversion of Jacob Coons in 1825 had been a demonstration of his understanding of the process of becoming a Christian after the New Testament order. In 1826 a concerted effort on the part of Smith and John Coons had resulted in a clear statement of the position of the dependable Spencer Creek Church.

During this time, as Smith's boldness in attacking critical points of Baptist doctrine began to result in some unrest among the churches, some of his friends attempted to persuade him to moderate his approach. He was warned that dire consequences could result should he persist in his revised course.

"Your more influential Baptist brethren," they said, "will abandon you; you will get nothing for your preaching; your debt will press you to the earth; and your farm and home must eventually be given up."

Smith's reply was indicative of his deep commitment to his determined course. Without equivocation he responded:

> Conscience is an article that I have never yet brought into market; but, should I offer it for sale, Montgomery County, with all its lands and houses, would not be enough to buy it, much less that farm of one hundred acres.[19]

During these eventful years, and regardless of the nature of his preaching, Smith's economic problems had persisted. He and his family experienced much hardship. This adversity was compounded by grief resulting from the death in 1822 of three-year-old William Pinckney, the third child born to him and Nancy.[20] Additional triumphs, defeats, and grief were imminent.

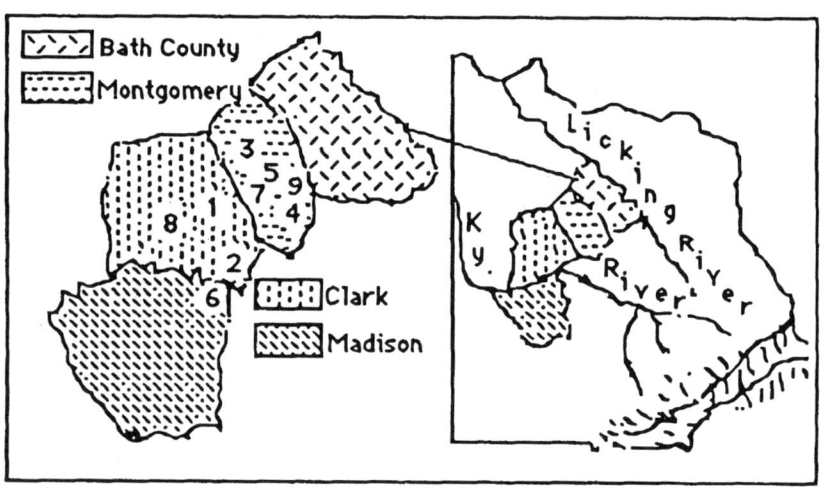

Annual meetings of North District Baptist Association were held at:
1, Goshen (1822); 2, Log Lick (1823); 3, Grassy Lick (1824);
4, Sycamore (1825); 5, Mt. Sterling (1826); 6, Cane Spring (1827);
7, Lulbegrud (1828); 8, Unity (1829); 9, Spencer Creek (1830).

CHAPTER 12

GUILTY AS CHARGED
(1827-1828)

LULBEGRUD REACTS

Opposition to John Smith's changing persuasions was slow in becoming organized. This was due to his growing popularity among the churches with which he was in close contact. However, after he withdrew as her preacher in 1823 his affiliation with Lulbegrud was essentially limited to a formal relationship with James French and the Lulbegrud messengers, whom he saw whenever the association convened to transact official business.

With the leadership of French, the messengers from Lulbegrud chose to formally express their opposition to the growing influence of a changing John Smith. It was the practice of each member church to prepare a letter and submit it to the association at the annual meeting. Lulbegrud's letter, prepared for the 1827 session, contained charges against Smith.[1]

By some means Smith learned that the charges were to be lodged against him when the association convened at Cane Spring in July of that year. It troubled him that his brethren clung so tenaciously to dogmas of human origin which prohibited the Scriptures from receiving an unbiased hearing. However, as much as he coveted their favor, he could not, in exchange for their good will, compromise what he believed the inspired record taught.

Compounding these concerns were anxieties he and his wife Nancy had carried for several weeks. A long illness had culminated in the death of Joshua Carroll, their three-year-old child.[2] He was buried on the day before the annual meeting. Of the first four children born to John and Nancy Smith, three were now dead.

Suspicious that opposition to him would be definitely and strongly expressed and that those whom he considered to be his friends would not support him, he requested that Nancy accompany him to the annual meeting. In addition to preferring not to leave his wife during a period of grief, he also felt a special need for her companionship during such difficult times. After arrangements were made for her brother to care for the children during their absence, Nancy yielded to her husband's request.[3]

Cane Spring was located slightly south of the Kentucky River in Madison County. David Chenault, the preacher at Cane Spring, was chosen as moderator and James French of Lulbegrud was again selected as clerk. Thomas Boone, as scheduled, delivered the introductory sermon. It appeared that the Calvinists were very much in control of the proceedings.

Clerk French chose not to reveal the contents of the Lulbegrud letter in the minutes of the 1827 meeting, but he did include:

> This association protests against any translation of the New Testament, except that translation of the New Testament in common use, and advises the member churches, to do so.[4]

Fortunately, another source preserved the Lulbegrud letter which detailed the charges against Smith. It indicated that one of the preachers had departed from Baptist usage in "several particulars," and further complained:

> That, while it is the custom of Baptists to use as the Word of God the King James's translation, he had, on two or three occasions in public, and often privately in his family, read from Alexander Campbell's translation.

> That, while it is the custom in the ceremony of baptism to take the candidate into the water, and solemnly pronounce the words, 'I baptize you, my brother, in the name of the Father and of the Son and of the Holy Ghost,' he, on the contrary, is in the habit of saying, 'By the authority of Jesus Christ, I immerse you into the name of the Father and of the Son and of the Holy Spirit.'

At this point, as the charges were being read, someone present interrupted and exclaimed that, "And there is no Ghost in it at all!"

The third accusation had to do with the administering of the Lord's Supper. It stated:

> That in administering the Lord's Supper, while it is the custom of the Baptists for an ordained preacher to stand at the table and give thanks, and break the loaf into bits, or morsels, small enough to be readily taken into the mouth, and then for the deacons to pass these around in a plate, or some like convenience, yet he leaves the bread in large pieces, teaching that each communicant should break it for himself.[5]

At what he deemed an appropriate time, Smith arose in the midst of what he regarded as a hostile audience and focused his attention upon the moderator.

"My brethren from Lulbegrud need not feel the least concerned for evidence to sustain their charges," he remarked to David Chenault in a tone of defiant humor, "I plead guilty to them all."

During a portion of the Saturday session and again on Monday, Smith vigorously defended his newly adopted positions. For reasons which the Calvinists later regretted, dealing with the heresy of John Smith was deferred until the following year.[6]

Because of an interesting combination of circumstances Smith was to deliver the introductory sermon at the next annual meeting. It had become the custom for that honor to pass to the current year's alternate. Since Thomas Boone had filled his appointment at Cane Spring in 1827, it was understood that alternate Smith would deliver the introductory address when the association convened at Lulbegrud in July of 1828.[7]

UNANTICIPATED VINDICATION

When the North District Association met at Lulbegrud in July of 1828, the crowd which gathered to hear the introductory sermon was so large that the meeting was moved from the building to a nearby grove.[8] According to the minutes, John Smith preached "from the 25th verse of the first, to the end of the second chapter of I Corinthians."[9] He can be envisioned on that occasion as stressing and applying in particular: "For I determined not to know anything among you, save Jesus Christ, and him crucified." In the language of the Scriptures, "Some believed the things which were spoken, and some believed not."

Since the hostile meeting of one year earlier, the North District Association of Baptists had, in effect, been "turned upside down." The membership at Spencer Creek, listed as one hundred forty-six in 1827, had grown to three hundred nineteen in one year. Grassy Lick had increased from one hundred twenty-six to two hundred twenty-three during the same period of time.

Having struggled during the years of controversy centered around emancipationist David Barrow, Mt. Sterling had grown from twenty-seven to a total membership of one hundred forty-two. People from the entire area were flocking to hear the preaching of John Smith. During this comparable time, when churches for which Smith preached enjoyed such phenomenal growth, Lulbegrud, Goshen, Cane Spring, and others whose history had been more Calvinistic in persuasion, declined in membership.[10]

During the latter part of 1827 and the first half of 1828 Smith relentlessly preached everywhere he could. In addition to filling his regular appointments at Spencer, Mt. Sterling, and Grassy Lick, it is recorded that he delivered at least two discourses every day. When churches with Calvinistic leadership closed their doors to him, he preached in groves, beside creek banks, in barns, and in houses.

Five new congregations had been established during the year, all termed "Reformer" churches. Messengers from these congregations, plus those who had been converted by Smith since the previous year, were so numerous that the Calvinists were outnumbered when the association met at Lulbegrud in July of 1828. Under such unanticipated circumstances the charges preferred against Smith the previous year were not mentioned.[11] A feeling of vindication accompanied him as he rode home from the meeting.

A TORRID PACE

Smith was home very little during the torrid pace of the first few months of 1828. As he hurried from place to place he often would stop only briefly for a short visit with Nancy and the children before proceeding on to the next appointment. On one particular occasion he rode his horse up to the yard gate and, without dismounting, called to his wife.

"Nancy," he said, presenting her the saddlebags in which he carried his clothing, "I have been immersing all week. Will you take these clothes and bring me some clean ones, right away? I must hurry on."

"Mr. Smith," she replied pleasantly, but with a touch of sadness in her voice, "is it not time that you were having your washing done somewhere else? We have attended to it for a long time."

"No, Nancy," he mused. "I am much pleased with your way of doing things, and I don't wish to make any change."[12]

The scope of the excitement generated by the preaching of John Smith permeated the entire Mt. Sterling and Montgomery County community. A letter dated April 20, 1828, from a father to his son who was attending school in Lexington, Kentucky, alluded to one of Smith's meetings. He wrote:

> ...a meeting in town today by Mr. Smith (Raccoon John Smith). There was 37 baptised, including Kenaz Farrow...old Jimmy Gatewood has a hope, J. Harvey Gatewood has been baptised. There is a great hope of some of the Harris family, but I am afraid a forlorn one.[13]

John Smith did not make a regular practice of keeping a journal. However, during a brief period of time in 1828 he made a few notes pertaining to his labors. To his wife he announced, "Nancy, I have baptized seven hundred sinners, and have capsized fifteen hundred Baptists."[14]

James Mason of Grassy Lick, a close friend of Smith for more than a decade, in a letter dated April 19, 1828, reported to the *Christian Baptist* that:

> he certainly is in himself a host, and the sectarian priesthood and their satellites have found it out, and are barking at him prodigiously; but the people are following him in crowds, and he is teaching them the ancient gospel with astonishing success.[15]

In the 1828 September issue of the *Christian Baptist*, Alexander Campbell reported:

> Bishop John Smith, of Montgomery County, Ky., who labors abundantly in the proclamation of the ancient gospel, has immersed since the 20th of April, till the third Lord's day in July, 294 persons. Thus, in a little more than 5 months, brother Smith has immersed 603 persons 'in the name of the Lord Jesus for the remission of sins.'[16]

Smith admitted that he had no idea that the Reformation, as the Restoration Movement was initially known, would prevail during his lifetime. However, since his frustrated sermon in 1822 and the pronouncement that he was "in the dark," he now felt that the struggle was essentially over. Having survived the difficult and decisive years of 1822-1828, he thanked God and his devoted wife, and resolved to continue in the course which had been established.[17]

CHAPTER 13

FAREWELL FROM THE BAPTISTS
(1829-1830)

Unfortunately, the minutes of the North District Baptist Association are missing for the years of 1829-31. Secondary sources, however, provide sufficient information to reconstruct a sequence of the significant events of that particular period. As a point of reference, 1829 is given as the date when the Baptists began separating from the Reformers.[1]

JAMES FRENCH AND LULBEGRUD COUNTERATTACK

The significance of James French in shaping the events which led to the Baptist separation from the Reformers in the North District Association cannot be overstated. Even though David Chenault of Cane Spring, James McDonald of Grassy Lick, and Thomas Boone of Lulbegrud were vocal, John Smith considered French "the wisdom of the opposition." The latter would quietly plan, while others, rather subconsciously, would execute his designs.[2]

During the 1829 annual association meeting at Unity, in Clark County, Smith encouraged the discussion of grievances expressed in correspondence from Lulbegrud and Goshen. The content of the letters complained of certain "heresies" which had permeated the association and expressed concern that their complaints had been ignored the two previous years at Cane Spring and Lulbegrud. Because they were in a minority, however, the Calvinists chose not to have the issues discussed on that occasion. David Chenault spoke in their behalf.

"Brethren," he bemoaned, "we can do nothing; for those who are complained against are more numerous than those who complain. There is only one course that is left to us, and that is, to withdraw ourselves from them."[3]

The disharmony of the Baptists resulted in a called meeting, initiated by James French, which convened at Lulbegrud in April of 1830. Attended by only seven of the twenty-five churches of which the district consisted at the time, it was resolved that the North District Baptist Association had departed from its constitution in "several particulars." These included the tolerating of departures from Baptist "customs" and "usage" of terms relating to the observing of the Lord's Supper, ordaining preachers, and using unacceptable terms in the administering of baptism. Likewise, there were other matters "so entire that to attempt an illustration throughout would be too long and tedious a writing."

Attention was called to one complaint in particular which apparently was especially annoying. It was stated that: "They even deny the special operation of the Spirit in quickening the dead sinner, and by way of ridicule they ask; 'Where did the Spirit hit you? Was it on the shoulder or under the fifth rib?'"[4]

Even though John Smith, by the nature of the invitation, had been excluded from participating in the called meeting at Lulbegrud, he chose to attend as an observer. Assuming that he would not be permitted to speak, he maintained his composure throughout the proceedings. As the session moved toward a conclusion, however, amidst confusion as to whether or not messengers should be sent to Spencer Creek for the annual meeting in July, Smith took advantage of an unanticipated opportunity to address the assembly.

During the discussion an "old Calvinist" who sat near Smith inquired of the latter his opinion concerning their going to Spencer. Apparently misconstruing Smith's response, the one who had sought his opinion arose and urged that the council meet at Goshen because the Reformers did not wish to see them at Spencer.

"Am I not right, Brother Smith?" he further inquired, expecting a positive response.

"No!" declared Smith, in a loud voice. "You are wrong on that, Brother Treadway, as you are in everything else!"

"What *did* you say?" retorted Treadway.

Detecting an opportunity to address the council at the same time that he replied to his antagonist, Smith rose to speak.

"Don't let him speak, Brother Moderator! Put him down! Put him down!" shouted someone from the floor to moderator Thomas Boone.

However, the intruder remained on his feet and scanned the audience as his countenance increasingly brightened. The frowns of those who comprised the assembly became more pronounced.

"Would you not let me tell the brother what I said?" inquired Smith.

A tumult resulted. Thomas Boone struggled in an attempt to maintain a semblance of decorum. Ultimately, by asserting himself with a voice louder than the protestors, he was successful.

"I decide," said he, "that Brother Smith ought to be allowed to explain himself; but he must do so in a whisper to Brother Treadway, who will then repeat it to the council."

"Whisper it again, Brother Smith," responded Treadway in a voice barely audible.

Still standing, Smith peered down into the upturned face of Treadway, and in a mock whisper, according to those present, spoke with sufficient volume to be heard by all within the house and by many who were outside the building.

"I said, Brother Treadway, that if you will all come to Spencer as brethren, we shall be glad to see you; but, if you expect to come there to padlock people's mouths, as you do here, you had better go anywhere else in all the world than to Spencer Creek! Now tell the moderator what I said!"

"You have *already* told it yourself, sir!" shouted the indignant Calvinist.

The council summarily adjourned with intentions to meet at Goshen in June of that year, one month before the Spencer meeting.[5]

JAMES MASON AND "THE PRESENT STATE OF AFFAIRS"

In May, the month following the Lulbegrud meeting and preceding the proposed Goshen Convention, James Mason penned his concerns to Alexander Campbell. Grassy Lick, the church to which he belonged, had experienced a division the previous year when a large group departed and organized the Somerset congregation. The letter, dated May 15, 1830, is quoted rather extensively because it so distinctly portrays the existing situation. Saddened by the events, Mason wrote:

> I feel greatly concerned on account of the present state of affairs in the religious world. This concern is increased from seeing those who I believe love the Saviour and love his people, arrayed against each other, as though Christ was divided and Paul was

crucified for them. At our last Association, although I had refused to be sent as a messenger from our church on account of the strife that existed in that body, my name was publicly read out as a heretic in a letter from one of the churches....But that which has destroyed the happiness I once enjoyed in society, is the schism that has taken place in the church where my membership is, on account of an old written creed, as old as the church itself, called the 'Church Covenant,' which held forth in 11 or 12 articles the old system of John Calvin, and which a majority of the church, with brother John Smith at their head, were determined no longer to put up with; and after voting it out they asked for letters, and constituted, in less than two miles where they meet, to themselves, and have as little to do with those they left as Jews and Samaritans.

...I am yet in the old camp, viewed with a jealous eye by both parties, and not very popular with either; and although my views as respects the gospel of Christ are pretty much in accordance with these reformers of yours, I am afraid to venture myself on board their boat, lest they run foul of a sawyer.

...The war seems at present to be waxing very hot, and I think this summer the great battle will be fought, which will drive every one to his proper stand. The North District Association has already had a swarm out of their hive. A foxy old man who has long been Clerk to that body, and had possession of her papers and records, has lately took it into his head to call a council of such churches as he thought would favor his designs, seven of whom attended by letter and messengers. These have, according to his designs, advised him to keep possession of the records of North District, and have appointed an Association to meet on the fourth Saturday in next month, and have invited all the churches or parts of North District Association that favor their designs, to meet them, and they will consider themselves North District Association....[6]

It will be recalled that James Mason was the Grassy Lick member with whom Jeremiah Vardeman corresponded in effecting arrangements for John Smith to move to Montgomery County. "The foxy old man" to whom he referred was James French.

The decision to separate had been initiated by the Baptists. They had hoped that the Reformers would depart, but it became evident to them that such was not going to happen. Therefore, to curtail the loss of individual members and, in many cases, majorities within congregations, the Baptists chose to sever all relations.

Believing that he could be more successful in converting both individuals and congregations by remaining within Baptist circles, John Smith continued to do so for as long as he could. This decision was a source of much vexation among the Baptists.

"Why is it," asked an impatient Calvinist on one occasion, "that you Reformers do not leave us? Go off quietly now, and let us alone."

"We love you too well to give you up," replied Smith. "It would indeed be a pity to part us."[7]

HISTORIC CONCOURSE AT SPENCER

When the majority of the churches of the North District Association assembled at Spencer in 1830 for the annual meeting, a few who had been very prominent within the district were conspicuous by their absence. Eighteen of the twenty-six churches, which composed the district the previous year, sent letters and messengers as usual. Lulbegrud and Grassy Lick were not represented.

Interestingly, Cane Spring, the location at which charges had been lodged against Smith three years earlier, sent her four allowable delegates. However, David Chenault, their determined leader for many years, was not among them. He remained at home with the minority of those who refused to be influenced by John Smith.

Thomas White of Beaver Pond (later Stanton, Kentucky) was selected as moderator, and Buckner H. Payne of Mt. Sterling was appointed clerk. Initially, Thomas Boone had been chosen to deliver the introductory address, but in his absence, John Newton Payne, brother of Buckner H., was given that assignment.

It was believed that in the history of the association a larger crowd had never before assembled within her boundaries. Present were prominent leaders of the new movement from within North District. Those from other districts included Jacob Creath, Sr., Jacob Creath, Jr., Josephus Hewitt, Josiah Collins, David S. Burnett and Thomas Campbell.[8]

Obviously, the most distinctive one among the group was the inimitable sixty-seven-year-old Thomas Campbell of Bethany, Virginia. It may be conjectured that his son, Alexander, perhaps had something to do with arrangements which sent his father to Spencer Creek. His presence would be a source of encouragement to those within North District who were struggling in their attempts to "speak where the Bible speaks, and to be silent where the Bible is silent."

Also present were representatives of the Somerset church, which was comprised of those who had departed the Calvinists at Grassy

Farewell From the Baptists

Lick. They were determined neither to be a part of any association nor to be known as a Baptist Church. However, when it was understood that association meetings would be converted into annual assemblies for Christian worship and communion, she sent representatives. [9]

With this meeting much consolation certainly came to John Smith. First, he was in extremely friendly territory. Spencer Creek had been more consistently supportive of his efforts to restore the ancient order than any of the other churches he served. Very early in his religious transition he had "anxiously wished for the day to arrive when all the congregations, like that at Spencer, would admit to baptism of a penitent believer on the simple confession of his heartfelt faith in Jesus." [10]

Second, the loneliness he had experienced in this same location eight years earlier when he declared that he was "in the dark" had been dispelled as many had come to share his aspirations. Now he felt neither alone nor rejected as had so often been the case.

UPPER SPENCER CHURCH OF CHRIST
The great 1830 "concourse" at Spencer Creek was conducted in a previous building located on the same site as the present one. It was erected on a beautiful knoll located on the William Ellis military land grant. The Calvinists refused to attend the meeting because they were outnumbered by the Reformers. However, such restoration giants as Thomas Campbell, Jacob Creath, Sr. and Jr., and David S. Burnett were present.

The first item of business at Spencer was an unpleasant one. John Smith and Buckner Payne were selected to prepare a written response to a document presented by representatives of the "Goshen Convention" which had met the previous month. In essence, the document again declared that "Baptist customs and usages" had been violated, and that North District Association had also "gone contrary" to her constitution in violating the Terms of Union of 1801. Near the end of the lengthy response, which dealt with each charge, Smith and Payne observed:

> Had the Goshen Council instructed their committee to examine the New Testament, in order to find what was enjoined by Christ, and practices by primitive churches and preachers, it would have shown that they intended to abide by the Terms of Union, which declare that the Word of God is our rule of faith and practice. But to appoint a committee to examine some unauthoritative documents, in order to find a set of human customs and opinions, looks more like violating the Terms of Union.[11]

After choosing Somerset as the location of the 1831 meeting, which was to be their last as an association, the historic assembly was adjourned.[12]

EXCLUDED AT ELKHORN

It is not to be supposed that the dissension which occurred during the spring and summer of 1830 was confined to the North District Baptist Association. Other associations within the state, many in which John Smith had preached, were experiencing the same type of cleavages. It is estimated that 10,000 Baptists had departed to cast their lot with the Reformers.[13]

Because John Smith was in attendance, it is appropriate to make special reference to the annual meeting of the Elkhorn Association which occurred on August 14, 1830, at Silas, Bourbon County, Kentucky. Convening two weeks after the great concourse at Spencer, the meeting included some of the best known names in the Baptist fellowship .

Silas M. Noel and Spencer Clack were among the six selected to preach. Noel was a force in the Franklin Association for many years, while Clack, of the Salem Association, eventually became well known in Missouri as well as Kentucky. Dr. Noel had much to do with the founding of Georgetown College in 1829, which was established primarily for the purpose of training Baptist preachers.

Also in attendance at the Elkhorn Association annual meeting were John T. Johnson of Great Crossings, Scott County, and Jeremiah Vardeman of David's Fork, located in Fayette County.[14] At this particular time Johnson was contemplating departure from the Baptists, while Vardeman, for approximately five years a part of the Reformers, had returned to the Baptist fold.

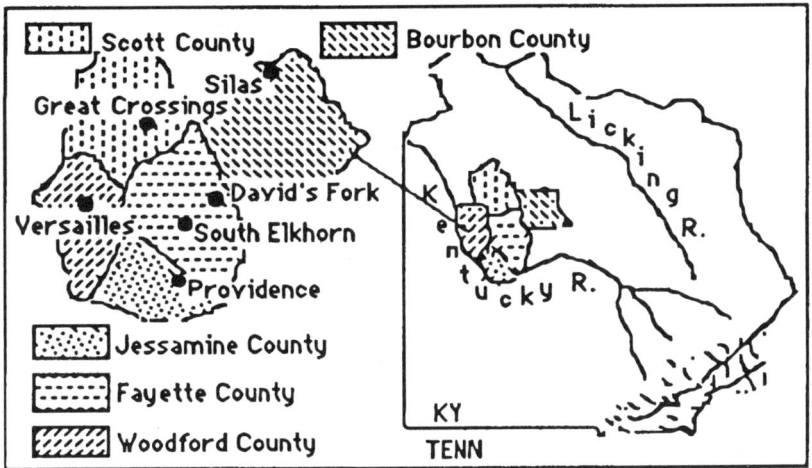

ELKHORN BAPTIST ASSOCIATION

Among the names of those serving as messengers and representing the churches within the bounds of the Elkhorn Association were Josephus Hewitt of South Elkhorn, located in Fayette County, Jacob Creath, Jr., of Providence, situated just south of the Fayette border in Jessamine County, and Jacob Creath, Sr., of Versailles. All three had been acknowledged by the Baptists as having joined the Reformers. The minutes indicate that each congregation represented by these three preachers submitted ten messengers for recognition. According to the apportionment ratio established by the association, each of these churches was entitled to a total of three.

Obviously, with previous knowledge that some type of action would be directed against them, the Creaths and Hewitt were attempting to have as many messengers seated as possible. These men, who were at the Spencer Creek meeting two weeks earlier, and the churches for which they preached, did not fare well at the Elkhorn meeting. Versailles and Providence were dropped from further correspondence with the association and a committee was "appointed to confer with the church at South Elkhorn, relative to certain grievances entertained against her, for having departed from the faith and constitution of this Association."[15]

John Smith, the acknowledged leader of the messengers of the majority group from North District,[16] was next. The record further states:

> It appearing that two communications from North District, have been sent to the Association showing that a split has taken place in that body:

> Resolved, therefore, that the ten churches who met in council at Goshen meetinghouse, on, the 4th Saturday in June, 1830, and in their Minutes declare that the balance of the churches have departed from her constitution, in faith and practice, be recognized as the North District Association; and that our correspondence be continued with her as heretofore.[17]

REFORM—A BAPTIST NEMESIS

It should be understood that those of Campbell's and Smith's persuasion did not initially intend to leave the Baptists. Their design was to redirect the convictions of entire congregations toward the cause of "Reform." It was this aspiration which deeply troubled those who intended to remain Baptists.

As they became more aware of what was happening, many determined Baptists such as James French, David Chenault, and Thomas Boone of the North District Baptist Association decided that a separation must come. Simultaneous movements were launched in other associations. Led by such preachers as Silas Noel, John Taylor, William Vaughn, Spencer Clack, and Walter Warder, the counter movements were designed to curtail the further loss of Baptist churches to the Reformers. What has been termed as a "civil war" resulted when the concerted counterattacks were launched.[18] Historian William Dudley Nowlin described the conflict from the vantage point of the Baptists. He wrote:

> Perhaps the reason for the strenuous opposition of the Campbellites to being separated from the Baptists was feeling that they could make proselytes faster being on the inside than they could being on the outside. And, too, they may have felt that by holding off the separation for a while they would have a majority in practically all the churches and thus exclude the minority and take possession of the property, as they did in a few cases where

they had the majority. The Baptists had to force the separation, and it would have been better for their cause had they forced it several years earlier.[19]

Until "Restoration" came to commonly designate the movement of those who sought to restore the ancient order, "Reformation" continued to be a primary motive. This was very evident in a report from an E. G. Benjamin on the Western Reserve, the designation of the northeastern quadrant of Ohio. It was published by Alexander Campbell in the May, 1843 issue of the *Millennial Harbinger*. Benjamin first enthusiastically elaborated upon the direction of reformation in his area of the Reserve, and then concluded by declaring: "Reform — reform — reform — let the word circulate until we come to the full stature of a man in Christ."[20] Indicative of his satisfaction with the article, Campbell promised a follow-up in the next issue.

EVERY MAN "TO HIS PROPER STAND"

James Mason had accurately predicted in his letter to Alexander Campbell four months earlier that, "I think this summer the great battle will be fought, which will drive everyone to his proper stand."[21]

With the called meeting by James French at Lulbegrud in April and the follow-up council at Goshen in June, the intentions of the Baptists were essentially announced. The climax of the conflict within North District had passed when, with the exception of the complaints lodged by representatives of the Goshen Convention, the Baptists boycotted the annual meeting at Spencer Creek in July. Beyond the district the turn of events at Elkhorn signaled to the Reformers of North District that there was no longer a place for them within the Baptist associations.

Before being "driven to their proper stand," Smith and his colleagues had gleaned every shred of every benefit possible from their continued association with the Baptists. As they rode home from the site of the Elkhorn meeting in Bourbon County, with the heat of the battle over, perhaps they were relieved in that they had "fought a good fight." Finally, the Baptists had bidden them farewell.

CHAPTER 14

JEREMIAH VARDEMAN—ENIGMATIC FRIEND OF JOHN SMITH
(1810-1830)

It will be remembered that John Smith, as a lad of twelve years, had first observed Jeremiah Vardeman playing the fiddle for a dance at Crab Orchard. Vardeman first befriended Smith in 1810 at the annual meeting of the Cumberland Baptist Association. As he became better acquainted with the country preacher from Horse Hollow, Vardeman perceived him as one of great potential.

When the devastated twenty-nine-year-old Smith returned from the scene of the Alabama tragedy in 1815, a letter of encouragement from his old friend, Jeremiah Vardeman, had resulted in his proceeding on to Crab Orchard and his preaching at "the stand." His memorable redemption sermon on that occasion assisted in thrusting him into influential circles which resulted in his becoming one of the most prominent preachers on the Kentucky frontier. Because of Vardeman's special interest in the young preacher and his having been responsible for also persuading him to go to the "destitute" churches of Montgomery County, his vehement opposition to Smith at the 1830 Elkhorn Association meeting appeared to be rather ironic.

THE BEGINNING OF THE END

It was not a total surprise for Smith to discover that Vardeman was aligned against him at the Elkhorn meeting. Having heard that his old friend was wavering in the cause of restoring the ancient order, Smith, in the fall of the previous year, had journeyed to David's Fork in Fayette County in an attempt to determine Vardeman's position. Upon arriving at David's Fork and hearing him preach, Smith's worst fears were realized. His old friend had indeed been lost to the cause.

Jeremiah Vardeman—Enigmatic Friend

A YOUNG AND AN OLDER JEREMIAH VARDEMAN
Reputed to have been an exceptionally handsome young man, as Vardeman advanced in age he became corpulent. He influenced John Smith to move to Montgomery County in 1817.

At the conclusion of Vardeman's sermon on that occasion, Smith boldly followed him to the pulpit and addressed both the audience and their preacher. He attempted to elicit from Vardeman a scriptural answer which would explain his return to the Baptists.

"As I desire above all things to know what is right, and to do it," Smith began, "I hope that Brother Vardeman will tell me, and this audience, what passage in the Word of God has convinced him that he was wrong. This I beg him now to do, not only for my sake, but for his own good, and that of the people."

"You know, my brethren," replied Vardeman, "how much I have always loved Brother Smith, for I have long known him to be a good man, and one that wants to stand in the truth of God. But to do what he now desires, would only lead us into controversy, and I do not wish to dispute about doctrinal matters with such a man as he."

After Vardeman's continued refusal to respond to his inquiries, Smith countered, "If now you do refuse to cite the proof that we are wrong, whom you so lately declared to be right, the people will justly conclude that you have abandoned us without any scriptural reason at all."

Declining further discussion, Vardeman promptly dismissed the audience.[1]

Because he knew well of the scriptural knowledge and exceptional skills which John Smith could bring to bear in a public discussion, Vardeman had no desire to be the object of Smith's probing in the presence of his David's Fork supporters. Relating this incident, Baptist historian Leo Crismon says of Smith, "Although he had a keen wit, it at times was consumed by his own brashness as demonstrated by his interruption of Vardeman's services to find out why he had left the reformers."[2]

At this juncture, it is believed that this account would be remiss should further attention not be given to John Smith's enigmatic friend. At the risk of redundancy and oversimplification an attempt will be made to analyze the ambivalent Jeremiah Vardeman who was an enigma in his own day to both the Reformers and Baptists.

A VACILLATING VARDEMAN

Jeremiah Vardeman was born in Virginia in 1775. When he was approximately twelve years old, his family migrated to the Kentucky frontier where he eventually became one of the best known preachers among the Baptists. After he and John Smith became acquainted, a warm friendship and mutual confidence existed between them for nineteen years. However, a vacillating Vardeman was responsible for the erosion of the common grounds which they shared.

After preaching for the Baptists for more than twenty years, Vardeman became fully aligned with the "Reformers" during the years of 1824-29. He abruptly changed positions, however, sometime during 1829, rejoined the Baptists, and migrated to Missouri the following year. It is believed that an examination and synthesis of Baptist and restoration literature establishes the basis for his defection.

William Vaughn, a contemporary of Vardeman and highly respected among early Baptist historians, obviously struggled in an attempt to explain the latter's ambivalence. He conjectured that Vardeman was, in fact, impressed with Alexander Campbell as a scholar more than he was committed to that which he taught. As stated in his opinion: "The high regard held for Campbell's scholarship made Vardeman and (Walter) Warder so tolerant toward reformation that they were accused, with some show of justice, of favoring its principles."[3]

From the time that Vardeman served as Campbell's moderator in the latter's debate with W. L. McCalla in 1823 there was no doubt but that he retained a high regard for Campbell. In fact, he is quoted as declaring: "If all the Baptist preachers in Kentucky were put into one, they would not make an Alexander Campbell." [4]

Vaughn is typical of other early Baptist historians who were cautiously critical of Vardeman's demeanor during the years of 1824-29. They were reluctant to charge him with anything more than simply going through a period of indecisiveness. Thomas M. Vaughn, biographer of his father, William Vaughn, states that Vardeman and Walter Warder, the latter an influential preacher of the Bracken Association, felt that:

> They could not beat back the tide that seemed to be sweeping all before it. They appeared to be paralyzed. They thought it would be more prudent to modify and direct the course of the reformation than to give it a direct and decided opposition.[5]

The younger Vaughn further asserted that their "silence had an unhappy effect" and that "during their silence more than half of the young and a multitude of the older church members had been carried away and they still were silent."[6]

Later Baptist historians continued to be reluctant to place Vardeman fully into the camp of the Reformers. Frank Masters chose to state: "Jacob Creath was completely won over to Mr. Campbell, and was among the first converts to the Reformation, Jeremiah Vardeman apparently wavered." [7] Baptist literature supports the proposition that as the interval of time which separates the present from the past becomes greater, the tendency to excuse Vardeman for his religious ambivalence during the critical 1820's also becomes greater.

IN THE REFORMER CAMP

Contrary to the contention of Frank Masters and others that Vardeman simply "wavered" are reliable sources which place him in full accord with the Reformers for perhaps as long as five years before his return to the Baptists. Richardson maintains that the renowned preacher was among the first in Kentucky to adopt a scriptural position with respect to baptism. He recorded:

> Jeremiah Vardeman, indeed, even from the time of the McCalla debate, had preached baptism for remission of sins with great zeal and effect. In November, 1826, he told Mr. Campbell that he had much more pleasure in immersing persons than formerly, before he was aware of the meaning of the ordinance.[8]

Another attempt by Baptist historians to escape the Vardeman dilemma is constructed around his reputation of having a disdain for controversy. J.H. Spencer observed: "He was not what is termed a doctrinal preacher, and still less a controversialist."[9] The implication appears to be that, in attempting to avoid controversy, he was simply misunderstood.

In the 1880's John Henderson Spencer served as the centennial historian for the Kentucky Baptists. During the nine years which he consumed in completing a two-volume account, he established his reputation as a meticulous researcher and reporter. Therefore, his objectivity should have been beyond question when he recorded: "Jeremiah Vardeman, by far the most popular and successful preacher in Kentucky, so far yielded to the new system about this time, as to baptize for the remission of sins."[10]

Spencer's heir apparent, bicentennial historian Leo Taylor Crismon, however, assumed the role of an apologist and presumed to lay the matter to rest by observing: "It was apparently his searching of the Scripture that led Vardeman away from the Reformation and back into the Baptist fold in the fall of 1829."[11]

VIEWING VARDEMAN FROM ANOTHER VANTAGE POINT

Any attempt to vindicate Jeremiah Vardeman becomes rather futile when further contrasted with other credible sources. First, there is no doubt about a measure of indecisiveness for which the Baptists mildly, but justly, criticize him. However, they fail to fully acknowledge that, when pressured to establish a position, this idiosyncrasy was compounded by a tendency to assume a posture for compromise.

An incident related by Jacob Creath, Jr., is indicative of this characteristic which was associated with Vardeman. Creath, Jr., accompanied by his uncle, Jacob Creath, Sr., visited him during the summer of 1830. Their primary purpose was to attempt to ascertain what course Vardeman intended to pursue at the decisive August meeting of the Elkhorn Baptist Association. Even though evasive pertaining to his intended course, he did reveal something of his persuasion at that time. Creath stated:

> We found that, to use his own complimentary phraseology, 'he intended to die between the Particular Baptists and the Christians, as our Saviour died between two thieves.' My uncle told him that 'If his old enemies, the Particular Baptists, caught him, they would

Jeremiah Vardeman—Enigmatic Friend

serve him as the old Canaanitish king, Adonibezek, treated his prisoners—cut off his thumbs and great toes, and make him eat bread under their table, all the days of his life; and if he fell into our hands, with whom he had formerly acted, he knew what we ought to do with him.'[12]

Consistent with his aversion to controversy, Jeremiah Vardeman had made it a practice to deal with themes which would engender very little doctrinal opposition. It is written of him that:

> In doctrine he was moderately Calvinistic. His views of the doctrine of atonement corresponded with those of Andrew Fuller in his 'Gospel worthy of all acceptation.' He delighted to defend the essential Divinity of the son of God; God's sovereignty and man's free agency and accountableness; the vicarious atonement of Jesus Christ upon the Cross, with all the other leading doctrines held by the denomination to which he belonged.[13]

Having become accustomed to the applause of the multitude, Vardeman preferred to strike a course in his preaching which was palatable to the majority. He discovered that the rigorous demands of restoration preaching would not accommodate this tendency. Under this yoke his capacity to endure was eroded.

Also, in addition to lacking the stamina to establish a position and stand firmly, Jeremiah Vardeman had difficulty in changing his preaching style from that which imparted Baptist doctrine to that which the Reformers believed to be scripturally sound. In an 1829 conversation with the Creaths, Vardeman alluded to financial concerns, but more significantly he revealed that he was not comfortable with the type of preaching which was generally employed by those involved in the "Reformation." His sentiments were paraphrased by Jacob Creath, Jr.:

> The preachers received but little money before the Reformation—they would have to get along on still less now. He intended to pursue his old course of text-preaching. He was too old to begin this chapter-preaching. He had heard him (my uncle) try it, and he had tried it himself, but neither of them succeeded like Morton, Gates, and the other young preachers.[14]

With this appraisal Vardeman accurately indicated a significant difference in styles of preaching which prevailed during that time. Indeed, a marked contrast existed between those of Vardeman's preferred style of evangelizing and that which was characteristic of diligent and courageous preachers who conscientiously aspired to restore first century Christianity. The literature portrays Vardeman as one who appealed almost exclusively to the emotion, while the Reformers delved into the Scriptures and attempted to use them to produce faith in the hearts of those who heard.

C. J. Conkwright explains that Vardeman's "forte was exhortation, and he could emphasize in the most pathetic manner the interjection, *Oh!* and could paint in living colors the happiness of the redeemed and the torments of the damned."[15] On the other hand, it is said of John Smith that his "style of preaching was in striking contrast with that of the clergymen around him. In exposition he analyzed the entire context, and carefully sifted whole chapters, comparing spiritual things with spiritual."[16]

Assuming that available sources are accurate, Vardeman, unlike Smith, admitted that he could not be comfortable attempting to conform to the exacting demands which were required in grasping the full scope of a text. The direction of his revised course was predictable when he announced that "he was too old to begin this chapter-preaching."[17]

Third, without unfairly placing Jeremiah Vardeman's motives under suspicion, there is evidence to suggest that he was rather sensitive concerning the source of his financial support. Crismon charges that it was "with tongue in cheek" that Robert Richardson, Campbell's biographer, quoted a conversation between Jacob Creath, Sr. and Vardeman. It is reported that as Vardeman was leaving the Reformers, he met Creath coming in the opposite direction.

'Hey Jerry, What's the matter?' inquired Creath.

'Oh,' replied Vardeman, 'If this thing takes, we'll all starve. The Baptists are not too liberal as it is.'[18]

Crismon's "tongue in cheek" charge does not take into consideration the scholarship of Robert Richardson. Evidence leads one to concede that Richardson was dealing with a matter of substance when he acknowledged that an "unsettled and discordant condition" had resulted in diminished contributions for preachers. As it pertained to Vardeman, Richardson believed that those prevailing conditions "were employed as a successful argument to retain in the Baptist ranks one who was a reformer in sentiment, and who had done much to promote the cause of the Reformation in Kentucky."[19]

John Smith was certain that Vardeman was very sensitive concerning his financial support. During one of his attempts to determine why Vardeman had defected, the latter's obviation revealed a questionable motive. Of a conversation between Smith and Vardeman, John Augustus Williams reports:

> 'But we profess to be governed by the Scriptures,' replied Smith, 'and we should be willing, if we are wrong, to be put down by the Scriptures. Where, then, is the proof that we are in error?'
>
> 'Brother Smith,' said Vardeman, evasively, 'you know how stingy the Baptists already are toward their preachers. But you will not get nothing at all for your preaching; you must all starve.'
>
> 'Still, you give me no proof that I am in error. Men have been martyred for the truth in times past; and, for one, Brother Vardeman, I would rather starve for its sake, now, than to fatten on error....' [20]

Fourth, an additional factor which contributed to Vardeman's discomfiture was an adversarial relationship with Jacob Creath, Jr. It was reported that resentment on the part of Vardeman toward Creath had developed when the Lexington Baptist Church invited Creath to become its minister. Vardeman had preached for the Lexington church during the years of 1827-30.

Because of the wide acceptance which he had enjoyed for many years, Jeremiah Vardeman was unaccustomed to dealing with competition. Creath observed that his inability to deal with the matter "laid the foundation of a deep and lasting hostility on his part toward me, which he exhibited on various subsequent occasions." [21]

Vardeman's animosity extended to others and worked much to his disadvantage. According to Robert Richardson, Vardeman, after his defection, believed it necessary to signalize his revived zeal for the Baptist cause. He chose to accomplish this objective by urging the most extreme measures against certain congregations "with a view of cutting off a few obnoxious individuals as the Creaths and Josephus Hewitt, who publicly advocated the primitive faith and order." [22]

John Smith, Vardeman's old friend of many years, was among the group which became the object of his scorn. As observed earlier, because of Vardeman's vehement objection during the 1830 meeting of the Elkhorn Association, Smith, along with the Creaths, was not permitted to defend himself after having been charged with failure to preach Baptist doctrine. Vardeman had reacted with anger when the proceedings had not gone as he preferred. Jacob Creath, Jr. reported in the *Millennial Harbinger*:

> Messrs. Vardeman and E. Waller acted in a very disorderly manner, calling upon the clerk to desist from reading them (letters from certain churches), and then upon the moderator to order him to do so. The Reverend Mr. Vardeman, failing to accomplish his purpose thus, rose with his cudgel in his hand, as if prepared to strike, and furiously remarked: 'Mr. Moderator! I *must* and I *will* be heard!' [23]

Rather than submit to an orderly discussion, Vardeman apparently had overreacted when developments failed to please him.

Fifth, even though he returned to the Baptists, Vardeman's vacillation not only resulted in some loss of confidence from the Baptist camp, but his return to them left him exceedingly vulnerable to the Reformers, whose numbers had increased to the point that he could avoid neither pressure nor controversy on any front. William Vaughn revealed the intensity of the pressure from the Reformers as he observed:

> The friends of Mr. Campbell were very busy in the dissemination of their principles. From the great leader at Bethany to the boy of fifteen summers there was unceasing activity. Every one of them was full of light and knowledge, and their hearts burned within them to communicate their doctrines to others. Whenever an opportunity presented itself, either in public or in private, they were discussing the topics suggested and developed in the *Christian Baptist*. They were as strong as Sampson, who slew a thousand Philistines with the jawbone of an ass; they felt that one could chase a thousand and two could put ten thousand to flight. [24]

Admittedly, there are some risks of oversimplification in attempts to analyze the complexities of Jeremiah Vardeman. However, as indicated by the factors which have been examined, there is little doubt but that in late 1829 he was in the center of a tempest which was testing his endurance.

Apparently the celebrated preacher was being assailed both from within and without. After having confronted Vardeman at David's Fork, Smith indicated that the audience "became suspicious" when their minister refused to give a scriptural reason for his transition.[25] His tenuous position was compounded when a division in the Baptist Church at Bryan's Station was attributed to him.[26]

There is also evidence to suggest that when the battle lines were finally drawn, Vardeman's Baptist defenders did not trust him in his reactions to the counterattacks of the Reformers. In his summation of Vardeman, J. M. Peck notes:

When assailed himself amidst the party conflicts that prevailed in Kentucky, he seemed never to think, as most men do, of the most successful means of self-defense. On such occasions, his most intimate friends and brethren would advise him to keep quiet, and they would defend his character from assaults. He was not a man...of controversy.[27]

EXIT VARDEMAN

The biennium of 1829-31 witnessed the climax of the struggle between those who intended to remain Baptists and those who were determined to pursue the course of restoring the ancient order. It may be conjectured that Vardeman initially perceived that in aligning himself with the "Reformation" he would be part of a cosmic drama destined to become the accepted course of the future. When he saw that a battle was on and that there would be two camps, he pitched his tent toward the one which best suited his temperament.

Jacob Creath, Sr. succinctly described the terminal point in recording:

> He set out in the Reformation before me; but, after I had enlisted under its banner, and started out to battle for it, I met my old comrade and brother, now disgusted and discouraged, coming home again, with his knapsack on his back.[28]

As one would suspect, Alexander Campbell deeply regretted the loss of Jeremiah Vardeman. He said of Vardeman's defection, "I knew him well, and if I had been in Kentucky at the time, Jeremiah Vardeman would never have been persuaded to abandon the cause of the Reformation."[29]

In 1830 the enigmatic Vardeman, at the age of fifty-five, abruptly migrated to Missouri. Baptist historians relate that he chose to move westward because Missouri held the promise of a larger farm that would better accommodate his family, which had become rather large by the addition of young children from a third marriage. However, factors previously related are believed to have influenced his decision to remove himself from the Kentucky scene.

J. M. Peck, a close confidant who met Jeremiah Vardeman at David's Fork in 1817, related:

> I renewed my acquaintance with him, and heard him again, under most favorable circumstances, at Edwardsville, Ill., in October, 1830. He was then moving from Kentucky to Missouri, with a family of about twenty-five persons,—old and young, and

travelling in Western frontier style, independent of taverns or hotels, and encamping out at night in the forest, or on the borders of the prairies. It was only at the urgent solicitation of friends that he could be induced under these circumstances, to attempt to preach.[30]

The Vardeman clan settled in Ralls County, Missouri, and "though advanced in years and grown corpulent," he was active in establishing and preaching for Baptist churches until his death in 1842.[31]

ENTER THOMAS HANSFORD

During 1830, the year in which Vardeman departed for Missouri, Alexander Campbell came to Kentucky on one of his preaching tours. Perhaps because of the influence of John Smith, Monticello and Wayne County were on his itinerary. Nestled in the valley along the Little South Fork of the Cumberland River in the southwest portion of Wayne County were John Smith's beloved Parmleysville and Horse Hollow.

It is not possible to conclude with absolute certainty that Campbell and Smith traveled together to Wayne County, but the history of Bethel Baptist Church at Parmleysville indicates that the latter returned there during the year of Campbell's visit. The records also reveal that in 1830 the membership "dropped to 30, probably as a result of the return of John Smith who split the church when about half of the members left and went with him."[32]

During Campbell's visit to Monticello a number of members of the Baptist Church were converted to the movement. Among them was Thomas Hansford,[33] the humble "unlettered country preacher" who had been responsible thirty years previously for the return of Jeremiah Vardeman to the Baptist fold after the latter had been expelled for his "worldliness." At the meeting of the Tates Creek Baptist Association in 1815 it was also Hansford who had persuaded the tattered John Smith to "mount the stand" in the grove at Crab Orchard.

Vardeman had been lost to the cause, but Thomas Hansford, his old mentor, had been gained.

VARDEMAN CEMETRY
The Vardeman family graveyard is located in an open field in Ralls County, Missouri.

The author is shown retrieving fragments of Jeremiah Vardeman's tombstone from beneath debris accumulated over many years. Vardeman died in 1842. Mike Weaver of Frankfort, Missouri, assisted in locating the grave.

CHAPTER 15

THE ROAD TO HILL STREET
(1823-1832)

A DECADE IN RETROSPECT

The third decade of the 1800's was by far the most eventful in the life of John Smith. Economically, he and Nancy had sacrificed beyond measure. Religiously, they had undergone a profound transition from Baptist doctrine to that which they sincerely believed to be a more scripturally tenable position. They had experienced rejection and endured periods of deep grief.

There were three children in the Smith family when the decade of the 1820's began. They were Jenny and Zerelda, daughters of John and Anne Townsend Smith, and little Jonathan, who had been born to John and Nancy in 1819, one month prior to the death of Eliza Blaze, their first born. Five more children, three sons and two daughters, were born during the 1820's. However, of the seven children born to Nancy, only four survived at the end of the decade. At this point in his life John had accompanied to the grave the remains of a wife and five of his eleven children.[1]

Smith faced the fourth decade of the nineteenth century with a feeling of having been liberated from the shackles of sectarianism. He had experienced much satisfaction in declaring that which he considered to be the order of the New Testament. No longer did he feel, as he had a decade earlier, that he was "in the dark."

In 1830 Smith was forty-six years old. He had now been in central Kentucky, and Montgomery County in particular, for thirteen years. Beyond the triumphs and defeats he had known during those years, there awaited another significant mission.

Reference has previously been made to the restoration initiatives of both Barton Warren Stone and Alexander Campbell. The

"Christians" of Stone's sphere of influence and the "Reformers" of Campbell's persuasion were destined to be formally united on January 1, 1832. John Smith considered his contribution to the effecting of that union as his crowning achievement.[2]

It is believed that two preachers served as quiet catalysts in bringing Smith to share the rostrum with Barton Stone at the Hill Street Church building in Lexington, Kentucky, less than two years after the Baptists had disassociated themselves from him. One of those preachers, John T. Johnson, was highly educated and well known in both public and religious circles. The other, Peter Hon, was of more humble origin and little known beyond a relatively small geographic area.

SCHOLARLY JOHN T. JOHNSON

John T. Johnson had been both a soldier and statesman. A veteran of the War of 1812, he carried to the grave marks of a wound received in that conflict. Following the war he prepared himself for a career in law. Eventually entering politics Johnson served both as a member of the Kentucky State Legislature and the United States House of Representatives. His brother, Richard, was elected a United States Senator in 1832 and began serving as Vice President under President Martin Van Buren in 1837.[3]

Born in 1788, the same year as Alexander Campbell, Johnson was said to have had "a lawyer's mind and a poet's heart." Perhaps because of his early commitment to military service and politics, it was relatively late in life when he turned his interest to matters of a spiritual nature.

Johnson was thirty-three years of age when, in 1821, he joined the Baptist Church at Great Crossings. During the years of 1829 and 1830, he brought his public life to a close so he could devote more time to his family.[4] Apparently unanticipated, his transition from public to private life was destined to be accompanied by a religious transition.

SMITH, JOHNSON, AND THE ELKHORN ASSOCIATION

The sequence of events involving John Smith and John T. Johnson, and which culminated in the formal union of the Stone and Campbell forces in 1832, had its inception during the previous decade. The acquaintance of Smith and Johnson was a consequence of contacts within the Elkhorn Baptist Association. Several years later, reflecting upon the events of the 1820's, Johnson acknowledged that he had known Smith as a Baptist preacher before he knew either Barton Stone or Alexander Campbell.[5]

A review of the minutes for the critical years of 1826-30 reveals that Johnson maintained a low profile during the annual meetings of Elkhorn, which convened on the second weekend of each August. At the time of the 1826 meeting Johnson was the preacher at Great Crossings in Scott County, Kentucky, and as often was the custom, served as one of the messengers at the association meeting. Surfacing that year was a problem between Elkhorn and the Licking Association. Licking charged that Elkhorn received "minorities of churches as the churches themselves."

In addition, and perhaps with significant implications, Licking asserted that she would:

> stablish correspondence with Elkhorn upon the 'inviolate maintainance [sic] of the Doctrine of Grace as revealed in the Bible, and set forth in the Philadelphia Confession of Faith (the constitution of each association) with the district understanding that each association will protest against any and every departure therefrom.'

The implications inherent within the condition reveal that basic Baptist doctrines were being assailed. The amiable John T. Johnson was chosen, with three others, to serve on a committee charged with the responsibility to resolve the existing problems.[6]

There is no record of John Smith being present at the 1826 annual meeting of Elkhorn, but he was very much in evidence the following year. On August 11, 1827, two weeks after being charged with heresy at Cane Spring, Smith appeared as a corresponding messenger from the North District to the Elkhorn Association meeting. Among those who accompanied him was John Coons, his colleague with whom he had drafted the Spencer Creek position paper the previous year.

John T. Johnson again served as a messenger from Great Crossings and was placed on a committee to assist in arranging the order of business for the following Monday. Nothing further is mentioned in the minutes concerning his participation. Although Johnson was not actively involved in the proceedings, he certainly was interested in a discussion which involved letters presented to the association from both the "First Baptist Church of Lexington" and the "Church of Christ on Mill Street." Dr. James Fishback was charged with leading in the change of the "denominative name" of the

Lexington Church, which resulted in "some distress" for both him and the church.[7] The controversial Fishback had a Montgomery County connection in that he was a brother-in-law of James Mason of Grassy Lick, a close associate of John Smith for more than a decade.[8]

Both Johnson and Smith were again present for the annual meeting of Elkhorn during the 1828 session. That was the year, it will be recalled, during which Smith had "baptized 700 sinners and capsized 1500 Baptists." While Johnson was very busy during the proceedings, Smith appeared only as a corresponding messenger from North District.[9] Beyond doubt, by that time Smith was becoming the object of much suspicion.

In 1829 John Smith was again present for the Elkhorn meeting. Surprisingly, after evoking the displeasure of many leading Baptists, he was among eight members "elected by private ballot to preach on Sunday." He was to speak to those who gathered in the Methodist meeting house.

Johnson, in addition to his role as a messenger from Great Crossings, was selected to serve with Jacob Creath, Jr. and Jeremiah Vardeman in the revision of a circular letter designed for churches within the association. Initially prepared solely by Jacob Creath, Jr., the letter was not accepted in its original form. When resubmitted, it was read and unanimously adopted. Johnson again had effectively served as a peacemaker.[10]

As previously indicated, John Smith attended the tumultuous 1830 session of the Elkhorn Association, but he and his colleagues were refused a place in the proceedings. According to the minutes, John T. Johnson did not serve as one of the messengers from Great Crossings that year.[11] Either he was too deeply involved in other matters to attend, or perhaps the kind and peace-loving Johnson had become weary of the contention generated in the defense of sectarianism.

During their contacts within the Elkhorn Association Smith and Johnson apparently formed a mutual respect. It also is certain that Johnson, as well as Smith, had diligently studied the issues which were presented in Alexander Campbell's *Christian Baptist*. In 1826 Barton Warren Stone began publication of the *Christian Messenger*.[12] Consequently, journals which presented the approaches of both Campbell and Stone in restoring the New Testament order were being circulated within the same geographic area.

Johnson was wise enough to understand the issues involved as the lines of fellowship were drawn. His type of involvement within the association as a peacemaker had kept him intellectually, as well as emotionally, above the petty wrangling. When the time came to make a choice, consistent with his temperament, Johnson could choose no other alternative than to cast his lot with John Smith and the Reformers. Consequently, when Smith was forced to part company with the Baptists, Johnson was not far behind in voluntarily doing so.

Acknowledging that he was too busy for several years to examine at length the tenets of the Reformation, he stated:

> During the years '29 and '30, I had more leisure. The public mind was much excited in regard to what was vulgarly called Campbellism, and I resolved to examine it in the light of the Bible. I was won over, and contended for it with all my might in the private circle. I was astonished at the ignorance and perversity of learned men, who were reputed pious, and otherwise esteemed honorable. My eyes were opened, and I was made perfectly free by the truth. And the debt of gratitude I owe to that man of God, A. Campbell, no language can tell.[13]

Soon thereafter Johnson was converted to the cause of the Reformers and immediately set about to convert the Baptist Church at Great Crossings. Unable to do so he formed a separate congregation in the same community with a determination to worship after the ancient order.[14]

A DELICATE MATTER—ENLISTING JOHN SMITH IN THE CAUSE OF UNION

Soon after his departure from the Baptists, John T. Johnson was befriended by Barton Stone, whom Johnson styled as "deservedly the most eminent preacher in the Christian connection in the West."[15] This friendship soon proved to be the necessary linkage in eventually bringing together the Christians of Barton Stone's movement and the Campbell-led Reformers. However, before such was accomplished, a key role awaited John Smith of Montgomery County.

It was difficult to bring Reformer Smith to the point where he was prepared to enter into a close fellowship with Barton Stone, his "Christian" neighbor immediately beyond the county line. The Baptists in North District were suspicious of the "Arians," especially those who resided in adjacent Bourbon County. Williams best described the chasm which had existed between them for a number of years. He recorded:

> Perhaps no two religious parties in the land, at that time, were further removed from each other by mutual prejudices, doctrinal

differences, and diverse customs than the Baptists and these Arians, or, as they were invidiously called, Newlights, or Stoneites. They differed from the Calvinists in their views of the Trinity, and of the nature, ground, and extent of the atonement. They had, besides, renounced all human creeds, and, for a quarter of a century, had been urging the union of all believers on the Scriptures as the only standard of faith and duty. They had refused to be called by any sectarian name, and had taken that of Christian, in the belief that it was the name divinely conferred on the disciples at Antioch.[16]

Further indicative of the hostility was a question concerning the Arians, which was presented to the North District Association at its 1828 annual meeting.

"Is it right to correspond with any association, that [sic] her churches hold Arians in their body, or commune with them?" the Salem Church inquired.

"*No*," was the unequivocal response.[17]

Even though Smith had enjoyed phenomenal success during that year in preaching a return to the ancient order, and had delivered the introductory address to launch the proceedings of the annual meeting, there is no evidence that he chose to contest the ruling. Apparently it did not occur to him as being of immediate significance. It was, however, indicative of the strong feeling against those who had been influenced by Stone.

In the fall of 1831 John Smith received an invitation from John T. Johnson to come for a meeting at Great Crossings.[18] There is no indication that Smith had any idea that the subject of union would be introduced during the visit. Such did happen, however, and Smith agreed to return to Georgetown in December for further discussions.

Beyond reasonable doubt, Smith was inclined to become involved in the Great Crossings and Georgetown discussions because of his brotherly commitment to his old friend of Elkhorn Baptist Association days. Nevertheless, despite Smith's respect for Johnson, it is believed that more than a hasty invitation from him was entailed in Smith's trek into Scott County for the purpose of discussing union of the Campbell and Stone forces.

There is reason to believe that a quiet, humble minister who preached for more than a half century in Montgomery, Nicholas, and Fleming Counties had much to do with the conditioning of John Smith to cross the "Demarcation Line" which separated Bourbon and Nicholas from the county of Montgomery. Attention is directed to him in the following chapter.

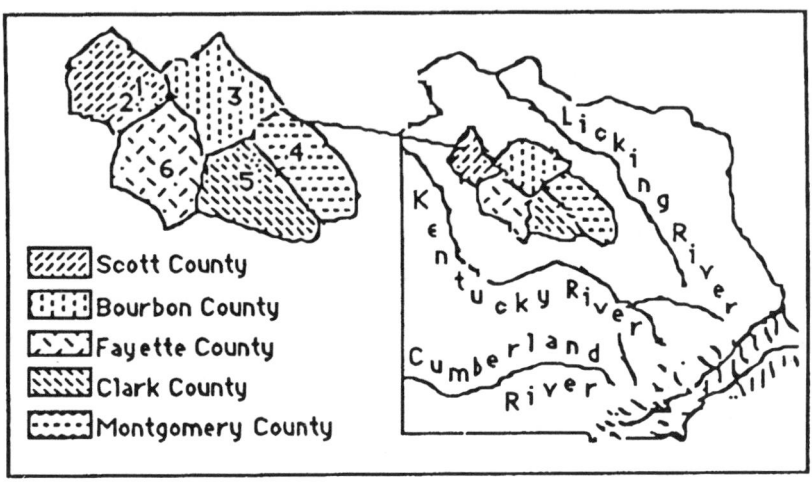

Fayette, Scott, and Bourbon Counties were within the Elkhorn Baptist Association while Clark and Montgomery were within the North District. Significant locations were: 1, Georgetown; 2, Great Crossings; 3, Cane Ridge; 4, Mt. Sterling; 5, Winchester; 6, Lexington.

CHAPTER 16

HILL STREET PRELIMINARIES
(1821-1832)

There were currents which both inhibited and contributed to union when representatives of the Campbell and Stone forces met at the Hill Street church building in Lexington on January 1, 1832. As will subsequently be related, the obstacles which inhibited union within John Smith's Montgomery County were much more apparent than those which contributed to it. Changing the Montgomery County context came neither easily nor quickly.

PETER HON—QUIET CATALYST?

Peter Hon, son of a Church of the Brethren minister, was born in 1791, the same year in which the Cane Ridge meetinghouse was constructed. His parents were members of a colony of German immigrants who had settled eight miles east of Cane Ridge in an area soon to become Nicholas County, Kentucky. Because of their views pertaining to immersion, members of the Church of the Brethren were commonly known as Dunkards. At the age of twenty, in keeping with their practice, Hon was baptized three times, face forward, and began preaching soon thereafter.[1] He was destined to become an effective advocate in the movement to restore the ancient order.

Two forces, one born from without and the other from within, shaped the course of Hon's life. First, since he was reared near the geographic center of Barton Stone's area of greatest influence, it is believed that he became a beneficiary of that influence.[2] Indeed, before continuing at Cane Ridge, the Great Revival of 1801 had actually begun at Concord, less than four miles from Hon's home. Second, his profound respect for the Scriptures led him to accept them as the exclusive authority in matters of religion. This attribute often had him at odds with the Church of the Brethren.

Reflecting upon the life of the humble preacher, a contemporary declared that Hon had always taken the Scriptures as his guide and quoted him as saying, "I have always contended that baptism was one of the means God has ordained for remission of sins."[3] By 1815 Hon was moving away from some of the basic doctrinal positions of the Dunkards. Soon thereafter he was branded as a heretic and expelled from the group.[4]

In 1824 Hon became the minister at East Union, Kentucky, his home community, and continued serving in that capacity for fifty-two years. Log Union, located north of the Licking River in Fleming County, listed him as their preacher for fifty years.[5] As was the general practice, the congregations were served on a rotating schedule.

TOWARD RESTORATION

In Kentucky Peter Hon was apparently the most important link between congregations of the Church of the Brethren and the Restoration Movement. After his departure from the Dunkards, he was successful in nurturing a number of dissident Brethren, eventually bringing them to accept the restoration plea.

From a biographical sketch prepared by the great, great granddaughter of Hon, it is related:

> At the association meeting in 1827 the Dunkers and the Baptists, who had now come together, agreed to call themselves just 'Christians.' After this date the Brethren Association ceased to function as a separate group and its leaders became public advocates of the Restoration cause.[6]

As previously related, the same year in which this sequence of events began, the North District Baptist Association had charged John Smith with preaching doctrine contrary to Baptist practice. These events, occurring ten years after Smith came to Montgomery County as a Baptist preacher, were significant because of subsequent contacts between Peter Hon and John Smith.

The confluence of ideas and events, which began merging in 1827, eventually formed grounds for more common understandings between Hon and Smith, and consequently, between those within their spheres of influence who were of the Stone and Campbell persuasions.

Hill Street Preliminaries

In 1822 Peter Hon established a "Church of Christ on the waters of Stepstone Creek." The original building was destroyed by fire and the present structure, shown here, has been abandoned for many years.

CROSSING "THE DEMARCATION LINE"

The northern boundary of the North District Baptist Association, formed during the early part of the 1800's, conformed to a line separating Bourbon and Nicholas Counties from the counties of Clark, Bath, and Montgomery. After 1804, the year of the "Last Will and Testament of the Springfield Presbytery" document, that boundary tended to become a partition between the Montgomery County Baptists to the south and the "Stoneites," or "Arians," to the north. The line continued to be observed even after a majority of the congregations of North District Baptist Association were converted by John Smith to the cause of the Reformers.

Extant records indicate that former Dunkard, Peter Hon, crossed the "Demarcation Line" into the territory of the North District Baptist Association and began propagating his restoration persuasions. By an old deed, dated 1833, it is known that as early as 1821 Hon organized a congregation on the waters of Stepstone Creek in Montgomery County. This group, if not immediately, very soon began to be designated as a Church of Christ. The exact statement within the deed refers to the "trustees of the Church of Christ constituted at the house of John Meyers by Peter Hon on the twenty-fourth day of March, 1821." [7]

After examining the terminology within the deed for the property on Stepstone Creek, Dr. R. L. Roberts, respected restoration historian, observed:

> The deed is of special interest because 'The Church of Christ' and 'Christians' are used as Stone used them. The proximity of East Union to Concord and Cane Ridge suggests the possibility of influence from men like John Rogers and Stone. Likely, Hon knew both of these men before any of them knew of the Campbells.[8]

It appears that the assumption of Peter Hon's Stone influence is sound, inasmuch as the establishment of the church on the waters of Stepstone Creek in 1821 predated by two years the first issue of the *Christian Baptist*. This observation is significant since Smith acknowledged that his Campbell influence first emanated from that publication.

The congregation established by Hon was located only about three miles from Smith's farm and four miles from his loyal Spencer Creek Baptist Church. It was already a year old when Smith confessed to the Baptist congregation at Spencer in 1822:

> Something is wrong — I am in the dark — we all are in the dark; but how to lead you to the light, or find the way myself, before God, I know not.[9]

Because of the lack of a detailed description, it is admitted that the exact nature of the congregation on Stepstone cannot be ascertained. Even though Hon had been formerly dismissed by the Dunkards, he continued to exert much influence among them, as evidenced by the 1827 merger of the Dunkards and a group of Independent Baptists. However, by the process of elimination, and in consideration of evidence that Hon had been influenced by Stone, the logical assumption is that he established on Stepstone Creek in Montgomery County a congregation similar to those of the Stone persuasion.

The discovery of the above mentioned document pertaining to the "Church of Christ on Stepstone Creek" somewhat alters the generally accepted view that the restoration initiative in Montgomery County was the exclusive consequence of John Smith's efforts as he was influenced by Alexander Campbell. Had the deed for the property on the waters of Stepstone not revealed the date of the work of Hon, his contribution most likely would have remained in oblivion, inundated by the phenomenal success of Smith in bringing the masses into the camp of the Reformers.

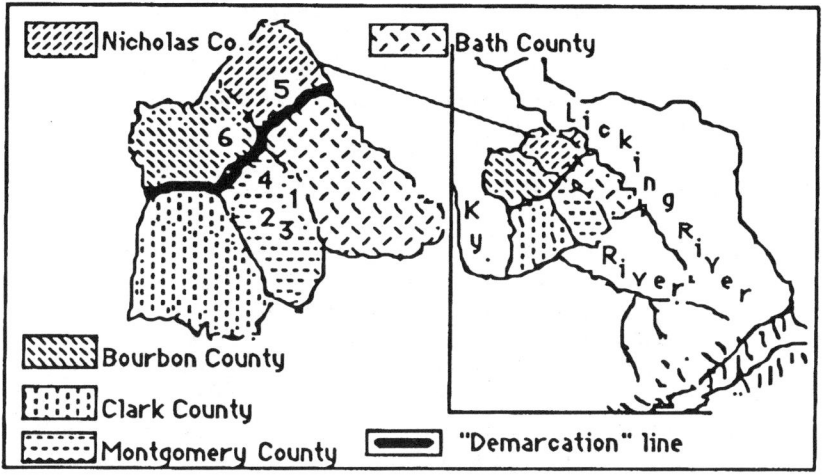

Bourbon and Nicholas Counties were considered to be the territories of Barton Stone and John Rogers until 1831. A de facto "line of demarcation" separated the Baptists of North District Association from the "Christian" territory to the north. Of significance is the fact that Peter Hon crossed into Montgomery County in 1821 and established a congregation on Stepstone Creek. Congregations contiguous to the area were: 1, Stepstone; 2, Mt. Sterling; 3, Spencer Creek; 4, Somerset; 5, East Union; 6, Cane Ridge.

THE GENTLE GERMAN AND THE BOLD COUNTRY PREACHER

From available information pertaining to Peter Hon it can be concluded that he was not an impulsive man who would "rush in where angels fear to tread." His love for the truth and the souls of mankind, complemented by a reserved and unassuming deportment, endeared him to those with whom he came in contact. His relationship with John Smith was no exception; as one examines his nature, his tendency to adopt a low profile and exert a quiet influence is readily understood.

Although it appeared somewhat later than the time under consideration, a report to Alexander Campbell in 1843 revealed much about the disposition of Peter Hon. He wrote:

> I have had a large family to raise, and my situation would not admit to extending my labors over a large scope of country. I have, therefore, labored in my immediate neighborhood and vacinity [sic]; and have been able, through the blessing of the Lord, to gather together and plant some seven or eight churches, all of which are in a flourishing condition, and walking in love....I have been the happy instrument of adding to the church, since April last, some five hundred persons. The Lord be praised, for the glory is due to him!

Alexander Campbell responded to the report by observing:

> I am happy in having formed a personal acquaintance with the excellent brother Hon and having heard, from testimony of the most satisfactory character, a report of his Christian excellencies, I can candidly salute him as a brother and fellow laborer in the Lord, and repose the utmost confidence in his statements.[10]

An examination of legal documents and bits of information from religious publications of the nineteenth century reveals that the gentle German and the bold country preacher of Montgomery entertained a mutual respect. Their common direction was consummated during the 1820's, well ahead of the formal joining of the Campbell and Stone forces. Subsequent examples are illustrative of the types of contacts which occurred.

First, the territories covered by Peter Hon and John Smith were not only contiguous but they often overlapped in a plurality of areas. Smith, as well as Hon, preached on the waters of Stepstone Creek.[11] Considering the fact that the valley of the Stepstone is a relatively small area, he undoubtedly was preaching to the same people to whom Hon had preached.

Second, extant records reveal that three of Hon's children married into the prominent John Coons family of the Spencer Creek congregation, where Smith preached regularly for thirty-three years. The Coons family had departed the Baptists with Smith, and Coons served as clerk of Spencer Creek Church for more than sixty years. Even though these marriages came after the 1820's, they indicate that there was much interchange of members of the Hon and Coons families among East Union, Stepstone, and Spencer Creek.[12]

Third, in July of 1831 Peter Hon and John Smith were together at Somerset, a Reformer church which was located three miles north of Mt. Sterling. The participants at this meeting concluded that they would meet no longer as a Baptist association.[13] With this development it may be assumed that without celebration a gradual union had taken place between Stone-influenced Hon and Campbell-influenced Smith. Perhaps the "few persecuted Arians" in the North District, to which reference is made by Smith's biographer, included Hon's Stepstone group in Montgomery County.[14]

Four months after the historic Somerset convocation, in November of 1831, Smith received the aforementioned invitation from John T. Johnson, his old friend of the stormy Elkhorn Baptist Association days, to come for a meeting at Great Crossings in Scott County, Kentucky. This meeting apparently provided for the first time an occasion for serious discussion with Smith concerning a possible union of the Campbell and Stone forces.[15] From a current vantage point, and considering his Montgomery County context, it is difficult to fathom the enormity of the task which confronted John Smith when he was encouraged to accept a leading role in that endeavor.

This observation can be appreciated more when it is remembered that even Alexander Campbell believed at the time that a union of the Christians and Reformers was premature.[16] On January 2, 1832, one day after the formal union, and before he knew of its consummation, Campbell published in the *Millennial Harbinger* a report of the Great Crossings meeting which had occurred in November of the previous year. In addition to expressing satisfaction concerning the "harmony and Christian love" which prevailed at the Crossings, he also noted that the same existed "between the disciples meeting under the Christian name in connexion [sic] with brother Stone in Georgetown."[17] The inference demonstrated his intention to keep the "disciple" designation in the forefront.

Following the commendations Campbell admitted that the relationship had developed "notwithstanding the sparrings between us editors," obviously referring to him and Barton Stone.[18] Had he known the details of the two meetings at Georgetown and Lexington which had transpired during the ten days prior to his writing his immediate reaction to what had happened would have been most interesting.

It may be conjectured that if Campbell had been in Kentucky at the time of the meetings, it is possible that union would not have come at the time it did. In that respect, it is very probable that in 1832 Smith assisted in attaining something which Campbell either would not, or could not, have accomplished.

Consequently, considering the climate at the time, and regardless of the characteristic courage and zeal of John Smith, it is believed that a primary source of prolonged influence and conditioning was necessary to bring him into this rapidly unfolding drama. The influence of John T. Johnson is readily acknowledged. Johnson was not in position, however, to support Smith within his hostile Montgomery County context.

Objectivity requires the acknowledgment of circumstantial evidence in some inferences which have been made with respect to Hon's influence within Montgomery County and upon John Smith. However, it appears that by orientation and geography Peter Hon had quietly served as a catalyst in bringing Smith and his Campbell influenced Reformed Baptist background into contact with Barton Stone of Bourbon and John Rogers of Nicholas County. The precise degree of the Hon influence cannot be determined at present.

Therefore, when Smith shared the platform with Stone at Hill Street in Lexington on January 1, 1832, it was the culmination of a lengthy orientation, rather than a quickly conceived notion.

PETER HON (1791-1876)

Peter Hon died in 1876 and was buried in the East Union Cemetry. His stone is located between the two small trees in the center of the picture.

CHAPTER 17

FORMAL UNION AND ITS WAKE
(1832-1834)

Among those attending John Smith's meeting at Great Crossings in November of 1831 were Barton Stone and John Rogers. Following the meeting John T. Johnson and Smith "conferred upon the general union of the churches" and the "importance and practicality" of that union. A second meeting followed in Georgetown, which "embraced Christmas day and afterwards," and a third began at the Hill Street building in Lexington on New Year's day, 1832.[1]

Soon after the Hill Street meeting convened, Smith was informed that he had been chosen to speak in behalf of the Reformers, and at Stone's suggestion, he also would be first in presenting his sentiments. History has judged that Smith rose to the occasion, which he deemed "the most important and solemn that had occurred in the history of the Reformation."

Feeling an immeasurable weight of responsibility pressing down upon him, he arose and began:

> God has but one people on the earth. He has given to them but one Book, and therein exhorts and commands them to be one family. A union, such as we plead for—a union of God's people on that one Book—must, then, be practicable.

He continued by observing that: "an amalgamation of sects is not such a union as Christ prayed for, and God enjoins." Speculative matters, he reasoned, should not be made a test of fellowship, inasmuch as they simply encourage a "wrangling spirit among my brethren." Declaring his allegiance "to the words of the Book," he concluded:

> Let us, then, my brethren, be no longer Campbellites or Stoneites, New Lights, or any other kind of lights, but let all come to the Bible, and to the Bible alone, as the only book in the world that can give us all the Light we need.

Stone followed with remarks which he considered appropriate for the occasion. In conclusion, he declared:

> I have not one objection to the ground laid down by him as the true scriptural basis of union among the people of God; and I am willing to give him, now and here, my hand.[2]

CALLED ON THE CARPET

The disappointment on the part of many in Montgomery and Bath Counties who had been among the first to be influenced by Smith was indicative of the skepticism which existed prior to the formal union of the Reformers and Christians. There was opposition at Somerset, but the opposition in Mt. Sterling was especially keen. Immediately after Smith arrived home, the elders of the Mt. Sterling Church went to his house and probed him concerning rumors they had heard. They envisioned serious consequences from what was regarded as "a grave blunder on the part of their father."

Opposition was also formidable in the neighboring Bath County communities of Sharpsburg and Owingsville. Regardless of his potential to anticipate the developing circumstances, Smith perhaps underestimated the reaction in the two counties where his efforts to restore the ancient order had begun. As would be expected, extant records reveal that there were no problems at loyal Spencer Creek.[3] Of the enormous task faced by Smith, John Rogers wrote:

> Brother Smith, my fellow-evangelist, was called to account, like Peter, for going in among our people & communing with them. It was charged in doing so, he was trampling upon the great principles of Union as taught by A. Campbell.[4]

In an attempt to assuage the opposition, Smith prepared an address for circulation in defense of the union of the Reformers with the Christians. His primary purpose in the address was to correct misrepresentations of Barton Stone and those whom he had influenced. The content dealt with the atonement, with the fellowshipping of the unimmersed, with opinions relating to the "character of Christ," with sanctioning the "sectarian speculations" of the Christians by breaking bread with them, and with the acceptability of the "Christian" designation.

Smith closed the address by appealing to the desire to "know the whole truth, and to practice it...as we think that the best of us, either as individuals, or as congregations, are not fully reformed, but reforming."[5] Of Smith's address, John Rogers remarked:

> The simplicity, the candor, the charity, the piety, the dignity and noble independence which this communication exhibits, are characteristic of the man who wrote, and, what is better, of the religion which he professes.[6]

SMITH AND ROGERS "TO RIDE"

In March of 1832 Alexander Campbell made reference to the developments in Kentucky. He quoted from the *Christian Messenger*, edited jointly by Barton Stone and John T. Johnson, the announcement that John Smith and John Rogers had been "separated" for a special mission. After acknowledging "the first known, *formerly*, by the name of Reformer, and the latter by the name of Christian," he stated:

> These brethren are to ride together through all the churches, and to be equally supported by the united contributions of the churches of both descriptions; which contributions are to be deposited together with brother John T. Johnson, as treasurer and distributor. We are glad to say that all the churches, as far as we hear, are highly pleased, and are determined to cooperate in the work.[7]

Perhaps two months after the union, Campbell's anxieties pertaining to it were subsiding. He rejoiced that they had "renounced their former speculations" and "that they now go for the apostolic institutions." Further, he believed that "from the present aspect of things, we have reason to thank God and take courage and to bid these brethren God speed." With exuberance he then declared:

> Reign, mighty King, forever reign,
> Thy cause throughout the world maintain;
> Let Israel's King his triumphs spread,
> And crowns of glory wreath his head![8]

The announcement that Smith and Rogers were "to ride" was not an overstatement. They indeed did ride! During the 1832-34 biennium, thirty-two reports pertaining to the missionary journeys of Smith and Rogers were published in the *Christian Messenger*. From the time of Campbell's announcement of their selections to travel in the interest of affecting the union, at least ten reports relating to their successful tours appeared in the *Millennial Harbinger*.

They traveled both together and separately, baptizing hundreds. Between them they ranged at least as far north as Georgetown, Ohio, and as far south as the Tennessee border. Their labors took them westward to the Green River country and eastward to the valley of the Big Sandy.[9]

Attempting to detail the two years of intense evangelizing by Smith and Rogers is beyond the scope of this account. However, it is appropriate to give attention to Montgomery and Bath Counties, the immediate area of Smith's residency. Likewise of particular interest are his visits to his boyhood home in Stockton's Valley and to Wayne County, his home before moving to central Kentucky. Between 1831 and 1834 Smith made at least three preaching tours to the area.

SUCCESS IN THE COUNTIES OF MONTGOMERY AND BATH

At the time of the union of the Campbell and Stone forces John Smith had lived in Montgomery County for fifteen years. While leading into the Restoration Movement the Baptist congregations at Mt. Sterling, Somerset, and Spencer Creek, he also was responsible for the establishment of additional churches in neighboring Bath County. During his far-ranging preaching tours, he did not overlook his immediate field of labor.

Smith was much loved by his brethren who knew him best. As they came to understand his purpose, they responded to and supported his preaching efforts. To the editor of the *Millennial Harbinger* on August 9, 1833, E. C. Payne of Mt. Sterling reported:

> Brother Smith has immersed near two hundred and seventy within the bounds of ten miles square, and not exceeding seven miles from his place. May the Good Lord continue to prosper his cause![10]

Thomas T. Swetnam, in a report from Bath County dated September 26, 1833, stated:

> We had a four days meeting at Upper White Oak, a few weeks ago; at which place a number of disciples met, with a large concourse of people. Great harmony prevailed throughout the

meeting. Between forty and fifty made the good confession; many more were very much shaken. Such a shaking of the dry bones of Calvinism I have never seen. Brother Smith exhibited the word each day, who is indeed himself a host. Our church constituted with eighteen members, five years ago. We now number about one hundred and twenty. We take the Book for our rule.[11]

A VISIT BACK HOME

Between 1831 and 1834 Smith made at least three trips to his home area in southern Kentucky. Because he had loved them in years past, he felt a special commitment to declare the ancient gospel to those to whom he had once preached the tenets of Calvinism. A report from Monticello, the county seat of Wayne, dated August 10, 1833, stated:

> The cause of reform is still progressing; we seldom meet but additions are made to the house of faith; at this time the number of names together are about 170, who are, with few exceptions, praising God and giving thanks for so great salvation.[12]

One year later, on August 19, 1834, from Monticello, Jonathan Frisbie reported:

> Brother John Smith has been recently among us. During his stay sixteen made the good confession, and were, by him, immersed into the apostolic faith. Shortly after his departure nine more were added to the congregation, and many more seem to be inquiring the way of the Lord. We number at this time about two hundred and sixty-five. The sects, especially the Methodists, are doing their utmost against us; but all their raving, ranting, perverting and falsifying avail them but little. Truth is mighty, and though but feebly advocated, will prevail.[13]

In a report bearing his Mount Sterling address and dated August 22, 1834, Smith revealed to John T. Johnson something of the extent of his travels during that particular tour. He wrote:

> A few days since, I have returned home from a tour of 32 days length. In which time I passed through several counties in this state as far down as Wayne and Cumberland. Thence through 6 or 7 counties in Tenn. Thence into Madison Co., Alabama.[14]

The tour into Alabama indicated that Smith continued to be mindful of those in Madison County, Alabama, who had endured with him the terrible tragedy befalling him there twenty years earlier. Of the area from southern Kentucky into northern Alabama, he continued:

> I can now assure you that the Christians in this section of the country, see but a small corner of the field, which loudly, loudly calls for laborers. In those parts, through which I have recently travelled, there are thousands of people who never have heard the gospel proclaimed in its primitive purity, and simplicity. The sects are completely buried in the rubbish of their own traditions; and sinners do not know what they must do to be saved, and (in many—very many places) there is no one to tell them. Hundreds are begging for someone to visit them, and teach them. I did not remain long enough at any one place to deliver more than one discourse except in two cases; and of course had not an opportunity of gathering much fruit. Notwithstanding all the disadvantages, 35 made the good confession in my tour. If you wish to see a complete moral waste, take a journey through that part of the country; and I think your spirit will be stirred within you, to see the people wholly given to sectarianism. Still the prospects for doing good are abundant and flattering. The great body of the people would hear and obey if they had the opportunity.[15]

On one of the visits to his home area Smith met Isaac Denton, the old Calvinist preacher who had baptized him into Clear Fork Baptist Church more than a quarter century previously. He inadvertently encountered Denton as he rode near Clear Fork. The two dismounted, sat together on a log, and engaged one another in a somber conversation.

"I suppose, Brother Denton," said John, "that you have heard many unfavorable things about me—concerning my departure from the faith, and the errors into which I have run."

"I have, Brother John," replied Denton. "I was grieved, deeply grieved, to hear them."

"Brother Denton," continued John, "you always professed that I was candid and truthful, even when a boy."

"I have always believed that, John," assured the grave old preacher.

"I hope, then," said Smith, "that you will think I am candid now, and that I will tell you the whole truth about my departure from the faith."

"Yes," replied Denton. "Satan has never tempted me to doubt that you were a Christian from the day that I baptized you to the present moment. But you are gone—you are gone, John!"

"Where to, Brother Denton?" quickly inquired Smith.

"From the faith of the Baptists," Denton countered as quickly.

"Well," replied John, "I will tell you truthfully the whole route I have traveled. I have gone from the Philadelphia Confession of Faith to the Bible as my only guide in matters of religion."

"I have set down Alexander Campbell, John, as the most erroneous and corrupt man in the world," charged the troubled old preacher.

The conversation soon ended and the two parted sadly, never to meet again.[16]

John next crossed the state line into Overton County, Tennessee, enroute to visit his ninety-year-old mother. Henry, the youngest son, had sold the old homestead in Stockton's Valley a decade earlier and his mother had gone to live with Elizabeth Matlock, a daughter.[17] As he approached the dwelling, she recognized him and tottered out to meet him.

After a period of embracing and allowing for unrestrained tears to subside, John led his aged mother into the house. Widowed for more than a quarter of a century, and although feeble in body, she still possessed a keen intellect. Subsequently, she revealed the distress which had resulted from her son's departure from the religion of his family.

"They tell me, John, that you have left us! They say that you deny the good Spirit that once gave you peace, and that you tell poor sinners that water can wash away their sins! For a long time I would not believe them. Why didn't you wait till your poor old mother was dead and gone?"

"Mother," he pleaded, "I confess that my mind has undergone some change in reference to the doctrines I once held as true, but many of the things that you have heard about me are idle tales. I do not teach nor believe such things. I have never denied the Spirit, nor taught that water can wash away sins."

"But, if you had only lived and preached as you once did, a few years longer, John, it would not have hurt me. I could have died so much happier," she sobbed.

"Mother, on your account," he added, desperately attempting to console her, "I would be glad if I were still a Baptist, but I could not, then, be true to my convictions of duty. It pains me, beyond expression, to wound the feelings of my mother, and I will now make you a fair proposition. I will turn back and preach Calvinism as faithfully as I ever did, for as long as you live, provided you will agree to answer for me in the day of judgment."

"Ah, John," she replied, "I can't do that. I shall have to answer for myself in that day, and so must you, my poor boy!"

"Well," he said, "if I must answer for myself then, do you not think, mother, that I ought to believe and act for myself now?"

Pondering the question, she wiped her eyes and replied, "I suppose you are right, Johnny. You ought to think for yourself. But you will have to account for it in the great day."

Even though she could not comprehend the nature of the apostasy of her son, she maintained until her death that she was not responsible for it.[18]

CHAPTER 18

THE END OF AN ERA
(1835)

The year of 1835 marked the end of an era in the life of John Smith. This was indicated, primarily, by the fact that the kind of intensive evangelistic endeavors he had known for eight years had come to a close. Six of those years had been diligently applied to "reform" within Baptist Churches. More than two years had been consumed with fellow laborer John Rogers in efforts to cement the union of the Reformers and Christians.

Rogers announced in April of 1835 that, because of dependent children and the failing health of his wife, his presence at home had become a necessity. Therefore, he would cease serving as a traveling evangelist. In October of the same year Smith likewise chose to tighten the geographic parameters of his preaching field. Encouraged by the Mt. Sterling Church to remain closer to home, he declined the invitation to serve in other areas of the state, and chose instead to confine his efforts primarily to the counties of Montgomery, Bath, and Clark.

Despite the limitations which Smith imposed upon himself, seven churches, and perhaps eight, continued to depend upon him. Spencer, Somerset, and Mount Sterling were within Montgomery County. Smith probably was responsible for the conversion of those who organized what is presently known as Antioch Christian Church, also in Montgomery. The deed to the Antioch property, dated September 8, 1834, conveyed to:

> the appointees by the Church of Christ a certain parcel of land to build a meeting house and containing one acre and a half situated and lying in the county of Montgomery on the waters of Little Slate....[1]

The End of an Era

It is further recorded that "the Antioch Church was first organized by a Joel Parker and Samuel N. McCormick, ministers, on the 5th day of May, 1833."[2] Even though Smith's name is not mentioned in extant records, the congregation, which met east of Slate Creek, was in the area where he had baptized hundreds of people. It is logical that these converts would have organized themselves into a congregation rather than cross the creek and journey an additional three miles to the Spencer Creek Church.

Upper White Oak, Owingsville, and Sharpsburg composed the Bath County circuit. In Clark County he continued with Bethlehem, located immediately beyond the western border of Montgomery County and organized the same year as Antioch.[3] The official records of the church state:

> On Saturday the thirty-first of August, 1833, the Church of Jesus Christ at New Bethlehem in Clarke County, Ky. was constituted into a congregation by the brethren John Smith, Jacob Creath, Jr., Joseph Collins and Orville Collins. The congregation agreed to adopt the New Testament as the rule of their faith and practice.[4]

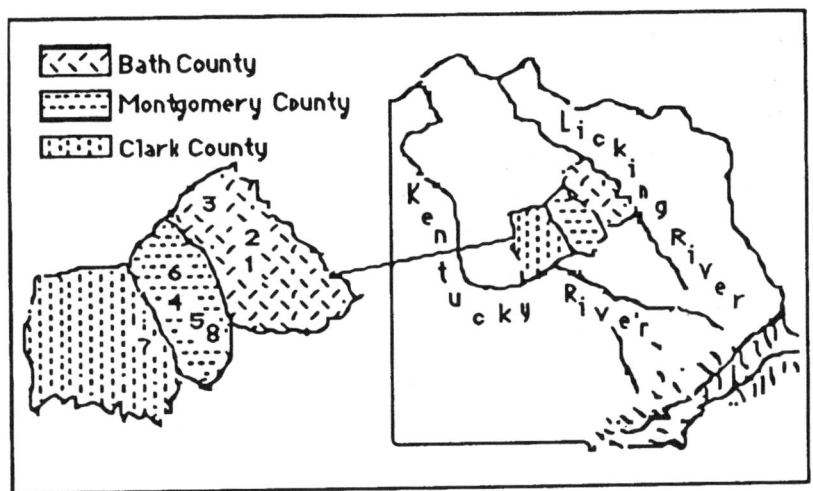

CHURCHES SERVED BY JOHN SMITH IN 1835
1, Owingsville; 2, Upper White Oak; 3, Sharpsburg; 4, Mt. Sterling; 5, Spencer Creek; 6, Somerset; 7, New Bethlehem; 8, Antioch.

RELIEF FOR NANCY

Smith's return to his role as a farmer-preacher provided another indication that an era had closed. For a decade his devoted wife had sacrificed beyond measure while he gave himself essentially to full-time evangelism. She was most deserving of some relief from the burdens of farming and the responsibility of caring for the children in the absence of her husband.

The size of the family continued to increase. Three births between 1831 and 1834 had brought the number of their surviving children to a total of seven.[5] Smith, now fifty years of age, certainly was aware that there was a need for him to give more attention to the rearing and training of his children.

In addition to the small children born to Nancy and him, were John's two grown daughters from his marriage to Anne Townsend. Very little is known about them except that one attended Philip Fall's school for girls in Frankfort in 1833.[6]

FAREWELL TO AN OLD ADVERSARY

Accompanying the end of an era for John Smith was the death of an old adversary who had epitomized the opposition during Smith's years as a Reformer. On April 1, 1835, James French of Lulbegrud died. As previously indicated, Smith had considered the old Calvinist to be the "wisdom of the opposition."

The name of French had been synonymous not only with the Lulbegrud Church but with the Calvinist opposition of the whole of the North District Baptist Association. Equipped with a keen mind, excellent training, and the experience gained by having served as a judge, he quietly and effectively used other people to accomplish his objectives. Indeed, he was regarded as one of the most accomplished among capable leaders on the Kentucky frontier.

The accomplishments of members of his family testified to the exceptionally high academic standards espoused by James French. Two of his sons were lawyers; one daughter was married to a physician and another to a judge. Furthermore, two grandsons became lawyers and another, John Bell Hood, was a highly regarded Confederate general.

At some point prior to the death of his old adversary John Smith went for a final visit with him. Perhaps the last time the two had been in a formal setting together was during the tumultuous meeting at Lulbegrud in April of 1830. The meeting had been called by French for the purpose of preserving Baptist Churches from the "wiles" of Smith. As the life of the hardened old Calvinist ebbed away, Smith chose to say to him:

> We have often been thrown in collision, Brother French, but I have no unpleasant recollections of anything you ever said to injure or to wound. You talked but little; but I used to think that you devised many things. I do not say this, now, to criminate you, in the least; on the contrary, I want you to feel assured that I have not an unfriendly feeling toward you in this world.[7]

The nature of French's response to Smith's kind remarks is not known. A decade earlier, when Smith began speaking of the need for reform, French favored limited reform within Baptist Churches, but he desired that they remain Baptist after reformation. When he became cognizant of the consequences of reform as Smith applied it, he considered the zealous young preacher more of a revolutionist than a reformer. He chose to fight rather than to see Baptist Churches destroyed in the reformation process.

In September of 1834, approximately seven months before his death, the old judge prepared his last will and testament. Indicative of his concern for family members was the fact that he prefaced the will with: "May the blessings of the most high be with all my descendants till time shall be no more." Included in his instructions was a wish that they press to a conclusion a battle he had waged for approximately seven years.

French's daughter, Keziah, named for her mother, had died in 1827 at the age of twenty-three while giving birth to her second child. Following her death, apparently a custody battle involving William French Prewitt, her first born son, had resulted in acrimonious skirmishes between her father and James Prewitt, her surviving husband. Before concluding the will, the terminally ill old patriarch instructed his family:

> The suit against James Prewitt be prosecuted to a decision in the appellate court and whatever may be recovered against James Prewitt, etc....[8]

The old veteran apparently could not die in peace without another campaign in process at the time of his demise. As the end of an era came for John Smith, one is tempted to conjecture that fate had made the end come as well to his old adversary who was responsible for the process of reformation coming at a higher price than should have been necessary.

THE GRAVE OF JAMES FRENCH
A cow grazes in the French family cemetery. James French's grave is in the center of the picture; that of Kaziah Callaway French, his wife, is to the right.

"INDEFATIGABLE" JOHN SMITH OF MONTGOMERY

Although he attempted to remain closer to home, Smith made two lengthy trips during the transitional year of 1835, one of which was to Louisville. He had learned that Alexander Campbell was on one of his tours through Kentucky and was scheduled to be in that city. While there he was in the company of Tolbert Fanning and Dr. Theodore S. Bell, as well as Campbell. Making reference to Smith's visit, Campbell observed: "We had the pleasure of being saluted in Louisville by our indefatigable brother John Smith of Montgomery [and others]." [9]

Smith's high regard for Alexander Campbell continued to remain intact during his entire lifetime. It is evident that whenever Campbell came into Kentucky, the "indefatigable" Smith attempted to be in his presence. His prevailing esteem of Campbell had been revealed the previous year, when, in providing an estimate of one who spoke of "meeting and celebrating" with the Bethany scholar, he wrote:

> Now, it does put me in mind of a fly rushing into a candle, for such men as myself, or John Wilson, to talk about meeting and celebrating with Alexander Campbell; even if we had ten times the learning and talent we have.[10]

In September of the same year Smith was in New Castle, Henry County, Kentucky. B. F. Hall reported in the *Millennial Harbinger* a meeting in which he and William Morton had preached, and stated that in the effort they had been "aided a few of the last days by brethren J. Creath, sen. [sic] and J. Smith." The fact that "seventy-five citizens of the neighborhood were immersed for the remission of sins" testified to the effectiveness of the endeavor.[11]

Further indicating the end of an era is the fact that no further reports of Smith's activities appeared in the *Millennial Harbinger* for a period of three years.

CHAPTER 19

AN OVERVIEW
(1836-1868)

POST MERIDIAN OF LIFE

During the transitional year of 1835, after eighteen years of residing in Montgomery County, John Smith sold his farm and relocated in the neighboring county of Bath. Since it made no significant difference in the area served by him in his preaching, it is difficult to ascertain the reason for his change of residence. The decision was probably based upon both economic and religious factors which are difficult to accurately reconstruct. It is unlikely that the precise reasons will ever be known, but nonetheless, there is adequate basis for rather sound conjecture.

First, the durable veteran of the cross may have felt it expedient that he make a geographic change. For a decade Montgomery County had been somewhat of a battleground of religious strife as Smith attempted to reform existing orders. Without implying that he ever avoided conflict at the expense of what he deemed to be right, at the same time it is logical to believe that a change of climate would have been refreshing to him and his family.

Second, apparently the economy was such in the 1830's that he was able to sell the Montgomery County farm for an amount sufficient to invest in considerably more acreage located in an adjoining county. Extant legal records reveal that within a period of less than three years John Smith purchased three tracts of choice Bath County land.[1]

For approximately thirteen years John and Nancy Smith resided in Bath County. While there he continued to maintain a close relationship with the Montgomery County churches. Because Bath borders Montgomery his new residence was only about ten miles from each of the three congregations in Montgomery where he preached.

In 1849 John and Nancy Smith chose to return to Montgomery County, this time within the city proper.[2] The prosperity experienced in Bath County enabled them to purchase a charming dwelling situated on more than three acres of land conveniently located near the business section of town and the church buildings where John preached. Sharing his time primarily between Mt. Sterling and Somerset, Smith, now sixty-five years of age, enjoyed an ideal living arrangement.[3]

Unfortunately, the apparent ideal circumstances for the old veteran of many campaigns were not to last. Much unrest resulted when William P. Clark, an over-ambitious and unscrupulous young preacher, came into town and waged a campaign of distrust against him.[4] The climate became so disconcerting that in 1851 Smith chose to sell his Mount Sterling property and relocate in Georgetown, Kentucky. He was soon exonerated by the Mount Sterling brethren, however, and in subsequent years returned often to preach.

During the 1850's Smith preached for various congregations in central Kentucky. There is evidence that he purchased a fine house in Georgetown and was more comfortable financially than at any previous time in his life.

Nancy Smith died in 1861, ten years after the move to Georgetown. John, who at the time of her death was seventy-seven years old, spent the remainder of his life frequenting the homes of his two daughters. Maria Lee of Owingsville, Kentucky, and Emma Ringo of Mexico, Missouri, were exceptionally attentive to their father during his declining years.

The last visit on record by John Smith to Montgomery County was in 1865, when he, in the eighty-first year of his life, preached at his beloved Spencer.[5] The country preacher from Wayne County's Horse Hollow continued to declare the good news of the kingdom of God through the last Lord's Day of his earthly life.

The inimitable John Smith died at the home of a daughter in Mexico, Missouri, on February 28, 1868. His body was returned to central Kentucky, the cradle of the Restoration Movement, where it was interred in the Lexington Cemetery.

THE "RACCOON" COGNOMEN

Perhaps it has become evident that the "Raccoon" diminutive commonly associated with the name of John Smith has not been apparent in this account. This approach has been deliberate, inasmuch as it is believed that its use is not compatible with the usage during the time frame under consideration.

Distinguishing one John Smith from another has more than likely been a challenge for every generation. The employment of "Raccoon," however, was not commonly used during Smith's lifetime to designate the venerable pioneer. Rather, within the bounds of Wayne County, "John Smith of Horse Hollow" was enough to identify the country preacher of Bethel Baptist Church at Parmleysville. Beyond the county "John Smith of Wayne" was sufficient.

The "Raccoon" cognomen had its origin in 1815 when Smith spoke at the annual meeting of the Tates Creek Baptist Association at Crab Orchard, Kentucky. An attempt to properly identify himself as being "from where the raccoons make their homes," appears to have been the beginning of his name being prefaced by "Raccoon." Smith charged that Jacob Creath, Sr. and John Davis, a Baptist preacher who lived in Crab Orchard, were responsible for an appellation which he did not prefer.

In a letter to a Samuel McKay, dated February 4, 1835, approximately twenty years following the date of the Crab Orchard meeting, Smith made reference to the origin of "Raccoon." The letter, bearing the caption of "Mr. Samuel McKays [sic] fibber corrector," dealt with several of what Smith considered to be significant misrepresentations by McKay. An excerpt from the letter, with punctuation unaltered, states:

> Into these matters we will now inquire and first in attempting to detail the conversation which took place between you and myself at your house in 1816 you say that I told you this, 'that the people of this neighborhood had given him the name of Raccoon Smith.' This is a mistake the people of my neighborhood nor of my County ever did give me that name the circumstance from which that name took its rise originated in the Crab Orchard, Lincoln County, between old Jacob Creath and John Davis a baptist preacher who lived in that place, and I am sure that no man in Wayne City had ever heard anything about it at the time I visited your house in the year 1816 and therefore I am certain that I never did tell you or any other person that the people of my neighborhood had given me the name of Raccoon Smith.[6]

He further held Philip Fall responsible for publicizing that to which he referred as "my ugly name." Fall had chosen to use "Raccoon" in advertising a meeting in which Smith would be preaching in Frankfort, the state capital. Smith related that the legislature was in session at the time and that all but four representatives from across the state had come to hear him. He contended that after the legislators were exposed to the "Raccoon" cognomen, they returned to their local districts and spread the name across the Commonwealth.[7]

"A THOUSAND PLEASING MEMORIES"

Whatever the circumstances which resulted in the "Raccoon" diminutive, "John Smith of Montgomery" apparently was the most used and his preferred identifying designation. The literature does not appear to support the unique distinction as being widely used immediately after the meeting at Tates Creek, nor does it often appear in the extant records which have to do with his long association with the Montgomery County churches. The high regard that people had for "John Smith of Montgomery," or "Elder John Smith," and often just simply "Brother Smith," evidently had them forego the slightest indignity that might have been associated with that "ugly name." Apparently Smith came to accept it but never to appreciate it.

Whatever the case with respect to his name, John Smith was a very common name affixed to a most uncommon and unpretentious man. Driven by motives as pure as those of an innocent child, he became extraordinary in his pursuit to restore the ancient order of things as they pertained to the kingdom of God. When Smith was eighty years old, it was said of him:

> He is generally and justly regarded, by those who have been acquainted with him, as one of the most remarkable men which the religious controversies of the present century have brought before the public, in the state of Kentucky.[8]

A source from his native Sullivan County, Tennessee, regards him as "the rarest human product that ever sprang from the soil of Sullivan County." The same source further states:

> He was tried by the severest tests of time; he was scourged by a living death, but with a masterful courage and unwavering devotion to the call of duty he arose to a rank that made him a

power throughout great portions of Kentucky, Tennessee and the Middle West....Along with Shelby, Clay and Boone, Smith has left an imperishable impress upon the State of Kentucky.[9]

It is believed that every accolade ascribed to Smith in life, and assigned to him since his death, have all been well placed. Four years before the death of the great preacher, it was observed:

> The trembling veteran of the Cross exhibits, to a marvelous degree, the active and powerful mentality of his earlier years. A thousand pleasing memories cluster around the name of R****** JOHN SMITH in the hearts and homes of the multitudes who have listened with rapture to his words of truth, being made glad in the consciousness of the pardoning favor of God.[10]

Attention is directed to two features of the above quotation. First, apparently the author had reservations about ascribing "Raccoon" to one of such singular stature. The distinguishing character of the name is simply indicated by an "R," followed by an asterisk for each letter. Second, he envisioned "A thousand pleasing memories" clustering around the name of the renowned subject of his sketch. More than a century later those pleasing memories continue to prevail.

NOTES

CHAPTER 1

1. Jack Ferguson, *Early Times in Clinton County*, 2 Vol. (Albany, Kentucky: by the author, 1986), Vol. I, 34.
2. John Augustus Williams, *Life of Elder John Smith* (Cincinnati: R. W. Carroll and Co., 1870), 11-13.
3. Winthrop S. Hudson, *Religion in America* (New York: Charles Scribner's Sons, 1978), 24.
4. Ibid., 25.
5. Williams, 12.
6. Charles Flinn Arrowood & Frederick Ely, *The Development of Modern Education* (New York: Prentice-Hall, Inc., 1946), 128-29.
7. J. Henshall, "Calvinism and Arminianism," *Millennial Harbinger*, Vol. III, Series III, No. VI (1846): 324.
8. Ferguson, Vol. I, 24.
9. Williams, 15-16.
10. "Awakenings in U.S.," *Christian History*, Wheaton, Ill. (Issue 23): 13-18.
11. Ibid.
12. The Arthur S. DeMoss Foundation, *The Rebirth of America* (Published by the Arthur S. DeMoss Foundation, 1986), 54-55.
13. Loulie Latimer Owens, *Saints of Clay—The Shaping of South Carolina Baptists* (Columbia, S. C.: R. L. Bryan Co., 1971), 22-26.
14. *Encyclopedia of Southern Baptists*, 2 Vol. (Nashville: Broadman Press, 1958), 1188.
15. Ferguson, Vol. I, 38.
16. John A. Garraty, *The American Nation* (New York/London: Harper & Row, 1971), 158.

CHAPTER 2

1. Jack Ferguson, *Early Times in Clinton County* (Albany, Kentucky: by the author, 1986), 38.
2. Lewis Preston Summers, *History of Southwest Virginia* (Baltimore: Regional Publishing Company, 1971), 120.
3. Robert Baylor Semple, *History of the Baptists in Virginia* (Printed 1810; revised 1894; Reprint ed., Lafayette, Tennessee: Church History Research and Archives, 1976), 25.
4. Winthrop S. Hudson, *Religion in America* (NY: Charles Scribner's Sons, 1973), 44.
5. Summers, 117.
6. Ibid., 117-19.

Notes

7. Hudson, 118.
8. Summers, 118-19.
9. Harold McKnight Wilson, *The Tinkling Spring* (Fishersville, Virginia: The Tinkling Spring and Hermitage Presbyterian Churches, 1954), 221-31.
10. Semple, 11.
11. Frank S. Mead, *Handbook of Denominations* (New York/Nashville: Abingdon Press, 1951), 27.
12. Henry Mayer, *A Son of Thunder* (New York/Toronto: Franklin Watts, 1986), 156-57.
13. Semple, 29-54.
14. J. H. Spencer, *A History of Kentucky Baptists*, 2 Vols. (Printed for the Author, 1886; reprint ed., Lafayette, Tennessee: Church History Research and Archives, 1976), Vol. 1, 194.
15. Ibid., 28-29.
16. Alice J. Hall, "James Madison, Architect of the Constitution," *National Geographic Society*, Vol. 172, No. 3 (September 1987): 350-51.
17. Mayer, 160.
18. Semple, 32.
Note: Semple believed that Patrick Henry did serve as counsel for one or more imprisoned Baptist preachers in Caroline County, but he questioned the authenticity of the account as given by Henry's biographer. He believed that it is was what J. M. Peck supposed Patrick Henry might have said under such circumstances.
19. John Augustus Williams, *Life of Elder John Smith* (Cincinnati: R. W. Carroll and Co., 1870), 12.
20. Ferguson, 38.
21. A. H. Newman, *History of the Baptist Churches in the Unites States* (Philadelphia: American Baptist Publication Society, 1898), 336.
22. Samuel D. Perry, *South Fork Country* (Detroit: Harlo Press, 1983), 154.
23. Williams, 11.

CHAPTER 3

1. John Augustus Williams, *Life of Elder John Smith* (Cincinnati: R. W. Carroll and Co., 1870), 17-29.
2. Robert L. Kincaid, *The Wilderness Road* (Middlesboro, Kentucky: Bobbs-Merrill Company in American Trails Series, 1947), 116.
3. James West Davidson & John E. Batchelor, *A History of the Republic*, 2 Vol. (Englewood Falls, N.J.: Prentice-Hall, Inc., 1986), Vol. I, 186-87.
4. Leonard Wood, Ralph H. Gabriel, & Edward L. Biller, *America: Its People and Values* (New York: Harcourt, Brace, Jovanovich, Inc., 1979), 165-66.

Notes

5. Ermina Jett Darnell, *Forks of Elkhorn Church* (Baltimore: Genealogical Publishing Co., 1980), 17.

6. Thomas Crittenden Cherry, *Kentucky - The Pioneer State of the West* (Boston: D. C. Heath and Company, 1935), 19.

7. "Warrior's Path, Wilderness Road" (*Cumberland Gap*, National Park Service; U. S. Department of the Interior).

8. James Lane Allen, *The Blue-Grass Region of Kentucky and Other Kentucky Articles*. (From compilation of articles first published in *Harper's* and *The Century* magazines, 1892; Lexington: King Library Press, University of Kentucky. Excerpts from the section: "Mountain Passes of the Cumberland," 1972), 2-3.

9. Thomas D. Clark, *A History of Kentucky* (Lexington, Kentucky: The John Bradford Press, 1960), 21.

10. Kincaid, 180.

11. Ibid., 142, 175.

12. Henry Thompson Malone, *Cherokees of the Old South* (Athens: The University of Georgia Press), 44-45.

13. Peter Cartwright, *Autobiography of Peter Cartwright* (1856; Rep. New York/Nashville: Abingdon Press, 1956), 5.

14. A. H. Redford, *The History of Methodism in Kentucky*, 2 Vol. (Nashville: Southern Methodist Publishing House, 1868), 68.

15. Kincaid, 198.

16. Ibid., 202-203.

17. John I. Rogers, *Autobiography of Samuel Rogers* (Cincinnati: Standard Publishing Company, 1880), 3.

18. Kincaid, 113-14.

19. Carl B. and Hazel Mason Boyd, *A History of Mt. Sterling, Kentucky, 1792-1918* (by the authors, 1984), 1.

20. Kincaid, 161, 164.

21. Darnell, 16.

22. George W. Ranck, "The Traveling Church," *Register of the Kentucky Historical Society*, Vol. 79, No. 3 (Summer 1981): 240-265.

23. S. J. Conkwright, *History of the Churches of Boone's Creek Baptist Association* (Winchester, Kentucky: By the Author, 1923), 18-21.

24. Everett Donaldson, Library of (Mt. Sterling, Kentucky: Collection of Historical Materials), "Sketch of Upper Spencer Church" file.

CHAPTER 4

1. "The Pennacle," National Park Service, U.S. Department of Interior, 2.

2. Ruben Powell, "The Jacksboro Road," (Berea, Kentucky: Unpublished paper, Weatherford-Hammond Mountain Collection, Berea College Library, 1979), 11-13, Attachment # 1, 4.

Notes

3. Samuel D. Perry, *South Fork Country* (Detroit: Harlo Press, 1983), 84-95.
4. Ibid., 96-99.
5. Jack Ferguson, *Early Times in Clinton County* (Albany, Kentucky: by the author, 1986), 11.
6. C. J. Puetz, *Kentucky County Maps* (Lyndon Station, Wisconsin), 28.
7. John Augustus Williams, *Life of Elder John Smith* (Cincinnati, R. W. Carroll and Co., 1870), 32-33.
8. Ibid., 13.
9. Ferguson, 38.
10. Ibid.
11. Williams, 31-32.
12. J. H. Spencer, *A History of Kentucky Baptists* (2 Vols. Printed for the Author, 1886; reprint ed., Lafayette, Tennessee: Church History Research and Archives, 1976), Vol. I, 234-35.
13. Ferguson, 36.
14. Charles L. Wallis, ed., *Autobiography of Peter Cartwright* (New York/Nashville: Abingdon Press, 1956), 30.
15. Ferguson, 36.
16. Williams, 41-42.
17. Perry, 154.
18. Louis Cockran, *The Frolic* (Lexington, Kentucky: The College of the Bible, 1964), 3.
19. Williams, 38.
20. Morris M. Gaskins, *A Lighthouse in the Wilderness* (Albany, Kentucky, The Clear Fork Baptist Church, 1972), 6.
21. Williams, 41-49, 62.
22. Ibid., 47.
23. Ibid., 48-64.
24. Gaskins, 34.
25. Ferguson, 36, 38-40.
26. Williams, 54.
27. Ferguson, 37-38.

CHAPTER 5

1. Jack Ferguson, *Early Times in Clinton County* (Albany, Kentucky: by the author, 1986), 38.
2. John Augustus Williams, *Life of Elder John Smith* (Cincinnati: R. W. Carroll and Co., 1870), 67.
3. Garnett Walker, *Exploring Wayne County* (Monticello, Kentucky: by the author, 1966), 3-4.
4. Ruben Powell, "The Jacksboro Road," (Berea, Kentucky: Unpublished paper, Weatherford-Hammond Mountain Collection, Berea College Library, 1979), Attachment # 9.

5. June Baldwin Bork, *Wayne County Kentucky Pioneers—Biographical Sketches and Civil Court Records* (Monticello, Kentucky: By the author, 1974), Vol 4, 73.
6. Williams, 67.
7. Walker, 5.
8. Williams, 67.
9. Ibid., 67-69.
10. *Dictionary of Quotations and Proverbs*, D. C. Browning, Compiler (London: D. C. Browning, Compiler, 1951), 67.
11. Williams, 69.
12. Ferguson, 37-38.
13. Williams, 70-74.
14. Louis Cochran, *The Frolic*, (Lexington, Kentucky: The College of the Bible, 1964), 44-45.
15. Williams, 74.
16. Ferguson, 40.
17. Williams, 75-76, 115.
18. Ibid., 77, 80-81.
19. Ibid., 90.
20. Ibid., 87.
21. Minutes, Bethel Baptist Church, (Monticello, Kentucky: Microfilm, Wayne County Public Library), Genealogy Section.
22. Ibid.
23. Bork, Vol 4, 73.
24. Williams, 88.

CHAPTER 6

1. Jack Ferguson, *Early Times in Clinton County*, 2 Vol. (Albany, Kentucky: By the author, 1986), 40.
2. John Augustus Williams, *Life of Elder John Smith* (Cincinnati, R. W. Carroll and Co., 1870), 96-97.
3. J. H. Spencer, *A History of Kentucky Baptists*, 2 Vols. (Printed for the Author, 1886; reprint ed., Lafayette, Tennessee: Church History Research and Archives, 1976), Vol. I, 263-64.
4. William Dudley Nolin, *Kentucky Baptist History*, 1770-1922, (Louisville: Baptist Book Concern, 1922), 40.
5. Samuel Eliot Morison, *The Oxford History of the American People* (New York: Oxford Press, 1965), 377-82.
6. Williams, 97-98.
7. Calvin D. Linton, Ed., *The Bicentennial Almanac* (Nashville/New York: Thomas Nelson, Inc., 1975), 75.
8. Ferguson, 40.
9. Williams, 99.
10. Survey maps, Public Library, Archives, Huntsville, Alabama.
11. "Taylor's History of Madison County," (Unpublished papers, Public Library, Archives, Huntsville, Alabama), 13, 45, 102.

12. Linton, 76.
13. Williams, 102-103.
14. Interview 3/12/90, Dot Johnson, Archivist, Public Library, Huntsville, Alabama.
15. *Holy Bible*, Jeremiah 31:15.
16. Williams, 108-109.

CHAPTER 7

1. John Augustus Williams, *Life of Elder John Smith* (Cincinnati: R.W. Carroll and Co., 1870), 110-12.
2. Ibid., 112.
3. Ibid., 113-14.
4. Ibid., 115.
5. Ibid.
6. J. W. Shepherd, *The Church, The Falling Away, and the Restoration* (Nashville, Tennessee: Gospel Advocate Co., 1948), 217.
7. Williams, 116-17.
8. Ibid., 119.
9. Ibid., 120-23.
10. Jack Ferguson, *Early Times in Clinton County* (Albany, Kentucky: by the author, 1986), 40.
11. Williams, 131, 133.
12. Minutes, Bethel Baptist Church of Christ, October, 1817 (Genealogy section — microfilm, Wayne County Public Library, Monticello, Kentucky).
13. Williams, 133.

CHAPTER 8

1. Carl B. and Hazel Mason Boyd, *A History of Mt. Sterling, Kentucky, 1792-1918* (By the Authors, 1984), 1, 3, 5.
2. Clarence L. Ver Steeg and Richard Hofstadter, *A People and a Nation* (New York/London: Harper & Row, 1977), 153, 186.
3. Everett Donaldson, Library of (Mt. Sterling, Kentucky: Collection of Historical Materials), "Old Fort Church" file.
4. J. H. Spencer, *A History of Kentucky Baptists*, 2 Vols. (Printed for the Author, 1886; reprint ed., Lafayette, Tennessee: Church History Research and Archives, 1976), Vol. 1, 260-263.
5. S. J. Conkwright, *History of the Churches of Boone's Creek Baptist Association of Kentucky* (Winchester, Kentucky: by the author, 1923), 71.
6. Spencer, Vol. II, 85.
7. Richard Reid, *Historical Sketches of Montgomery County* (Lexington, Kentucky: James M. Byrnes Company: for The Woman's Club of Mount Sterling, Kentucky, 1926), 10.

Notes

8. Frank M. Masters, *A History of Baptists in Kentucky* (Louisville: Baptist Historical Society, 1953), 167.
9. John Augustus Williams, *Life of Elder John Smith* (Cincinnati, R. W. Carroll and Co., 1870), 224-25.
10. Ibid., 286-90.
11. Boyd, 11.
12. Williams, 130, 134.
13. Ibid., 131.

CHAPTER 9

1. Jack Ferguson, *Early Times in Clinton County*, 2 Vol. (Albany, Kentucky: by the author, 1986), 40.
2. John Augustus Williams, *Life of Elder John Smith* (Cincinnati: R. W. Carroll and Co., 1870; reprint ed. Indianapolis: Religious Book Service), 136.
3. Minutes, North District Baptist Association, (Copies in library of Everett Donaldson; originals in Archives, Southern Baptist Seminary, Louisville, Kentucky), 1819-29.
4. Williams, 136.
5. Mary Lamberton Becker, ed., *Gulliver's Travels* by Jonathan Swift (Cleveland/New York: The World Publishing Company, 1947, original,1726), 104.
6. Richard Reid, *Historical Sketches of Montgomery County* (Read at the Fourth of July Celebrations, 1876; reprint ed., The Woman's Club of Mount Sterling, Kentucky; Lexington, Kentucky: James M. Byrnes Company, 1926), 39.
7. Everett Donaldson, "The Departed Glory of Lulbegrud," *The World Evangelist* (November 1987): 20.
8. Minutes, North District Baptist Association, 1816, 1817.
9. J. H. Spencer, *A History of Kentucky Baptists* (2 Vols. Printed for the Author, 1886; reprint ed., Lafayette, Tennessee: Church History Research and Archives, 1976), Vol. I, 260-61.
10. "Early Families of Montgomery County and Pioneer Kentucky—French Families," *Mt. Sterling Advocate*, 17 September 1975.
11. Spencer, Vol. I, 260.
12. S. J. Conkwright, *History of Churches of Boone's Creek Association* (Winchester, Kentucky: by the author, 1923), 71.
13. Williams, 135.
14. Spencer, Vol. I, 192, 196, 368.
15. Minutes, North District Baptist Association, 1823.
16. Calvin D. Linton, Ed., *The Bicentennial Almanac* (Nashville/New York: Thomas Nelson, Inc., 1975), 82.
17. Hazel Mason and Carl B. Boyd, Jr., *A History of Mt. Sterling, Kentucky 1792-1918* (Mt. Sterling, Kentucky: by the authors, 1984), 18.

18. Williams, 142.
19. Ibid.
20. Williams family genealogy (copy in library of Everett Donaldson).
21. Williams, 143.
22. Minutes, North District Baptist Association, 1819, 1820.
23. Ferguson, 40.
24. Williams, 145.
25. Ibid., 146.

CHAPTER 10

1. "Awakenings in the United States." *Christian History*, (Issue 23): 25.
2. John Augustus Williams, *Life of Elder John Smith* (Cincinnati: R. W. Carroll and Co., 1870), 44.
3. John B. Bowles, *The Great Revival. 1787-1805* . (Lexington, Kentucky: The University Press, 1972), 61.
4. John A. Garraty, *The American Nation* (New York/London: Harper & Row, 1971), 299.
5. Winfred Ernest Garrison, *Religion Follows the Frontier* (New York/London: Harper & Brothers, 1931), 65.
6. Robert Stuart Sanders, *An Historical Sketch of Springfield Presbyterian Church* (Frankfort, Kentucky: Roberts Printing Company, 1954), 28.
7. John Rogers, *The Biography of Elder Barton Warren Stone* (Cincinnati: for the author, by J.A. and U. P. James, 1847), 121.
8. J. W. Shepherd, *The Church, The Falling Away, and The Restoration* (Nashville: Gospel Advocate Co., 1948), 158.
9. Max Ward Randall, *The Great Awakenings and the Restoration Movement* (Joplin, Missouri: College Press Publishing Company, 1983), 62.
10. Garrison, 61.
11. Earl Irvin West, *The Search for the Ancient Order*, 4 Vols. (Nashville: The Gospel Advocate Company, 1949), Vol. I, 10.
12. Randall, 95-96.
13. "An Address to the Different Religious Societies, on the Sacred Import of the Christian Name" (Lexington, Ky.: printed by Joseph Charless, 1804; reprint, Lincoln College Press, Lincoln, Ill., 1969).
14. Randall, 75-76.
15. William Herbert Hanna, *Thomas Campbell—Seceder and Christian Unity Advocate* (Joplin, Missouri: Reprint. ed., College Press Publishing Company), 112-17.
16. Robert Richardson, *Memoirs of Alexander Campbell*, 2 Vols. (Philadelphia: J. B. Lippincott & Co., 1871), Vol. 1, 274.

17. Ibid., 396.
18. Alexander Campbell, "Prospectus," *The Christian Baptist*, Vol. I, No. 1 (July 1823): iv.
19. Richardson, Vol. 2, 200.
20. Williams, 428-430.

CHAPTER 11

1. Minutes, North District Association of United Baptists, held at Goshen Meeting house, Clark County, Kentucky, fourth Saturday in July, 1822 (Winchester, Ky.: printed by N. S. Finnell), copies in library of Everett Donaldson; originals in library of Southern Baptist Seminary, Louisville, Kentucky.
2. S. J. Conkwright, *History of the Churches of Boone's Creek Association of Kentucky* (Winchester, Ky.: by the author, 1923), 71.
3. Minutes, North District Association of United Baptists, 1823.
4. Robert Richardson, *Memoirs of Alexander Campbell* (2 Vols., Bethany, Brook County, Virginia: J. B. Lippencott & Co., 1871), Vol. 2, 108.
5. Alexander Campbell, "Prospectus," *Christian Baptist*, Vol. I, No. 1, (July 1823): iv.
6. Minutes, North District Association of United Baptists, 1824.
7. John Augustus Williams, *Life of Elder John Smith* (Cincinnati, R. W. Carroll and Co., 1870), 161-69.
8. Robert Richardson, *Memoirs of Alexander Campbell*, 2 Vols., (Philadelphia: J. B. Lippincott & Co., 1871), Vol. 2, 200.
9. Robert Stuart Sanders, *A Historical Sketch of Springfield Presbyterian Church* (Frankfort, Kentucky: for the author by Roberts Printing Co., 1954), 28.
10. Williams, 194.
11. Sanders, 113.
12. Williams, 194.
13. Ibid., 196.
14. Minutes, North District Baptist Association, 1825.
15. Ibid., 1817, 1826.
16. "The Coons Family" file. Library of Everett Donaldson.
17. "Upper Spencer Church of Christ" file. Library of Everett Donaldson.
18. Minutes, North District Baptist Association, 1826.
19. Williams, 198.
20. Jack Ferguson, *Early Times in Clinton County*, 2 Vol. (Albany, Kentucky: by the author, 1986), 40.

Notes

CHAPTER 12

1. John Augustus Williams, *Life of Elder John Smith* (Cincinnati, R. W. Carroll and Co., 1870), 180-81.
2. Jack Ferguson, *Early Times in Clinton County*, 2 Vol. (Albany, Kentucky: by the author. 1986), 40.
3. Williams, 180-81.
4. Minutes, North District Baptist Association, 1827. Copy in library of Everett Donaldson, originals in Archives, Southern Baptist Seminary, Louisville, Kentucky.
5. Williams, 183.
6. Ibid., 187-90.
7. Minutes, North District Baptist Association, 1827.
8. Williams, 252.
9. Minutes, North District Baptist Association, 1828.
10. Ibid., 1827, 1828.
11. Williams, 257.
12. Ibid., 238.
13. Carl B. and Hazel Boyd, *A History of Mt. Sterling, Kentucky 1792-1918* (By the authors, Mt. Sterling, Kentucky, 1984), 25.
14. Williams, 258.
15. Alexander Campbell, "Report from Churches," *Christian Baptist*, Vol. V (April 1828): 248.
16. Ibid., Vol. VI, No. 2, 47.
17. Williams, 259.

CHAPTER 13

1. S. J. Conkwright, *Churches of Boone's Creek Baptist Association of Kentucky* (Winchester, Kentucky: for the author, 1923), 28.
2. John Augustus Williams, *Life of Elder John Smith* (Cincinnati, Ohio: R. W. Carroll & Co.; reprint ed., Religious Book Service, Indianapolis, Indiana, 1870), 309.
3. Ibid., 297.
4. William Dudley Nowlin, *Kentucky Baptist History* (Louisville, Kentucky: Baptist Book Concern, 1922), 93.
5. Williams, 338-40.
6. Alexander Campbell, "Report from Churches," *Millennial Harbinger*, Vol. I, No. 6, (June 1830): 274-75.
7. Williams, 393.
8. Ibid., 353-54.

Note: Inasmuch as the minutes of the 1830 session of the North District Baptist Association are not extant, John Augustus Williams is the only known source for information on the Spencer meeting. Since his family was associated with the Somerset Church, some of his information could possibly have come from that source. Before their loss, he most likely had access to the minutes and probably had discussed the proceedings with John Smith. Williams, born September 25, 1824, was only five years old when the historic Spencer concourse occurred.

9. Ibid., 352-53.
10. Ibid., 217.
11. Ibid., 361.
12. Ibid., 362.
13. Frank M. Masters, *A History of Baptists in Kentucky* (Louisville, Kentucky: Kentucky Baptist Historical Society, 1953), 217-22.
14. Minutes of the Annual Meeting of the Elkhorn Association of Baptists, held at Silas, Bourbon County, Ky., Aug. 14, 1830, (Copy, Library of Everett Donaldson, original, Library of Southern Baptist Seminary, Louisville, Kentucky).
15. Ibid.
16. Nowlin, 94.
17. Minutes of the Annual Meeting of the Elkhorn Association of Baptists, Aug. 14, 1830 .
18. J. H. Spencer, *A History of Kentucky Baptists*, Vol. I & II (Printed for the author, 1886; reprint ed., Lafayette, Tennessee: Church History Research and Archives, 1976), Vol. I, 617.
19. Nowlin, 98.
20. Alexander Campbell, "News from the Churches," *Millennial Harbinger*, Vol. VII, No. 5 (May 1843).
21. Ibid., Vol. I, (June 7, 1830): 274-75.

CHAPTER 14

1. John A. Williams, *Life of Elder John Smith* (Cincinnati: R. W. Carroll and Co., 1870; reprint ed., Indianapolis: Religious Book Service), 312-13.
2. Leo Taylor Crismon, *Baptists in Kentucky, 1776-1976*, A bicentennial Volume, (Middletown, Kentucky: Kentucky Baptist Convention, 1975), 207.
3. Thomas M. Vaughn, *Memoirs of Rev. William Vaughn, D.D.* (Louisville: Caperton and Gates, 1878), 164.
4. Williams, 152.
5. Vaughn, 163.
6. Ibid., 165.
7. Frank M. Masters, *A History of Baptist in Kentucky* (Louisville: Kentucky Baptist Historical Society, 1953), 211.
8. Robert Richardson, *Memoirs of Alexander Campbell* (J. B. Lippencott and Co., 1871), Vol. II, 287, 324-25.

Notes

9. J. H. Spencer, *A History of Kentucky Baptists*, 2 Vol. (Printed for the author, 1886; reprint ed., Lafayette, Tennessee.: Church History and Archives, 1976), Vol II, 239-40.
10. Ibid. 98.
11. Crismon, 205.
12. Philip P. Donan, *Life of Jacob Creath, Jr.* (Indianapolis: reprint ed., Religious Book Service), 86.
13. J. M. Peck, "Rev. Jeremiah Vardeman," *Ford's Christian Repository*, Vol. VI, No. 23 (1854): 475.
14. Donan, 87.
15. S. J. Conkwright, *History of the Churches of Boone's Creek Association of Kentucky* (Winchester, Kentucky: by the author, 1923), 71.
16. Williams, 496.
17. Donan, 84.
18. Crismon, 205.
19. Richardson, Vol. II, 324-25.
20. Williams, 327.
21. Donan, 84.
22. Richardson, Vol II, 325.
23. Donan, 88-89.
24. William Dudley Nowlin, *Kentucky Baptist History* (Louisville: The Baptist Book Concern, 1922), 87.
25. Williams, 313.
26. Peck, "Ford's Christian Repository," Vol. VI, No. 32, (1854): 470.
27. Ibid., (page # illegible).
28. Williams, 423.
29. Richardson, Vol. II, 326.
30. Peck, "Ford's Christian Repository," Vol. VI, No. 32 (1854): (page # not legible).
31. Ibid., (page # illegible).
32. "A Brief History of Bethel Baptist Church," (Monticello, Kentucky: Genealogy Section, Microfilm, Wayne County Public Library), 3.
33. Masters, 220.

CHAPTER 15

1. Jack Ferguson, *Early Times in Clinton County*, 2 Vol. (Albany, Kentucky: by the author, 1986), 40.
2. Max Ward Randall, *The Great Awakenings and the Restoration Movement* (Joplin, Missouri: College Press Publishing Company, 1983), 277.
3. H. Leo Boles, *Biographical Sketches of Gospel Preachers* (Nashville: Gospel Advocate Company, 1932), 43.
4. John Rogers, *The Biography of Elder J. T. Johnson* (Cincinnati: for the author, 1861), 20-21.

5. Ibid., 24.
6. Minutes, Elkhorn Baptist Association, 1826. (Copies in library of Everett Donaldson, originals in Archives, Southern Baptist Seminary, Louisville, Kentucky).
7. Ibid., 1827.
8. John Augustus Williams, *Life of Elder John Smith* (Cincinnati, R. W. Carroll and Co., 1870), 231.
9. Minutes, Elkhorn Baptist Association, 1828.
10. Ibid., 1829.
11. Ibid., 1830.
12. Earl I. West, *The Search for the Ancient Order*, 4 Vols. (Nashville: Gospel Advocate Company, 1953), Vol. I, 234.
13. Rogers, 21.
14. Ibid., 22.
15. Ibid., 27.
16. Williams, 428-29.
17. Minutes, North District Baptist Association, 1828 (Copy in library of Everett Donaldson, originals in Archives of Southern Baptist Seminary, Louisville, Kentucky.
18. Dean Mills, *Union on the King's Highway* (Joplin, Missouri: College Press Publishing Company, 1987), 98.

CHAPTER 16

1. Mabel Lucas and Nancy Lucas Hampton, "Dunker Disciple," *The Disciple* (Feb. 1988): 17-19.
2. David B. Eller, "Peter Hon and the Kentucky Dunkards," *Messenger*, Vol. 136, No. 5 (May 1987): 18.
3. L. H. Reynolds, "Obituary," *The Apostolic Times*, Vol. VIII, No. 29 (July 1876): 460.
4. Lucas, 18.
5. Reynolds, 460.
6. Lucas, 19.
7. Deed Book No. 16, (Montgomery County Courthouse, Mt. Sterling, Kentucky), p. 234.
8. Letter, R. L. Roberts, September 9, 1988, (Hon file, library of Everett Donaldson).
9. John Augustus Williams, *Life of Elder John Smith* (Cincinnati: R. W. Carroll and Co., 1870), 145.
10. Alexander Campbell, "News from the Churches," *Millennial Harbinger*, Vol. VII, No. V (May 1843): 234-35.
11. Williams, 220.
12. Misc. Wills, deeds & marriage records, (Copies in Hon file, library of Everett Donaldson, Mt. Sterling, Kentucky).
13. Williams, 416-17.

14. Ibid., 448.
15. Dean Mills, *Union on the King's Highway* (Joplin, Missouri: College Press Publishing Company, 1987), 98.
16. Max Ward Randall, *The Great Awakenings and the Restoration Movement* (Joplin, Missouri: College Press Publishing Company, 1983), 280-81.
17. Alexander Campbell, "News from the Churches," *Millennial Harbinger*, Vol. III, No. I, (January 1832): 29.
18. Ibid.

CHAPTER 17

1. Dean Mills, *Union on the King's Highway* (Joplin, Missouri: College Press Publication Company, 1987), 98.
2. John Augustus Williams, *Life of Elder John Smith* (Cincinnati: R. W. Carroll and Co., 1870), 451-55.
3. Ibid., 461-63.
4. John Rogers, *The Life and Times of John Rogers, 1800-1867, of Carlisle, Kentucky*, transcribed by Virginia Bell, abridged by Roscoe M. Pierson and Richard L. Harrison, Jr. (Lexington, Kentucky: Lexington Theological Seminary, 1984), 86.
5. F.L. Rowe, ed., *Pioneer Sermons and Addresses* (Cincinnati: F. L. Rowe, 1908), 184-192.
6. Williams, 464.
7. Alexander Campbell, "The Christian Messenger," *Millennial Harbinger*, Vol. III, No. 3, (March 1832): 138.
8. Ibid., 139.
9. Williams, 463.
10. *Millennial Harbinger,* Vol. IV, No. 9, (Sept 1833): 432.
11. Ibid., No. 10, (October 1833), 526.
12. Ibid., No. 9, (September 1833), 474.
13. Ibid., Vol. V, No. 9, (September 1834), 473.
14. *Christian Messenger,* VIII, No 1 (January 1834):16.
15. Ibid.
16. Williams, 405.
17. Jack Ferguson, *Early Times in Clinton County* (Albany, Kentucky: by the author, 1986), 37.
18. Williams, 410-11.

CHAPTER 18

1. Deed Book 17, Courthouse, Mt. Sterling, Kentucky, pp. 6-7.
2. Brad Sorrell & Bruce Hills, "A Church History of Antioch Christian Church" (Mt.Sterling, Kentucky, 1965), 1.

Notes

3. John Augustus Williams, *Life of Elder John Smith* (Cincinnati, R. W. Carroll and Co., 1870), 530-31, 536-37, 546.
4. "New Bethlehem Christian Church," Clark County, Kentucky, Membership Rosters, 1833-1870 (Reprint ed.: Montgomery County Historical Society, Mt. Sterling, Ky., 1991), 5.
5. Jack Ferguson, *Early Times in Clinton County* (Albany, Kentucky: by the author, 1986), 40.
6. Williams, 513.
7. Ibid., 309-10.
8. Will Book D, Courthouse, Mt. Sterling, Ky., pp. 515-517.
9. *Millennial Harbinger,* Vol. VI, No. 7 (July 1835): 331.
10. *Christian Messenger,* Vol. VIII, (1834): 360f.
11. *Millennial Harbinger,* Vol. VI, No. 9 (Sept 1835): 441.

CHAPTER 19

1. Deeds - Three tracts of land (DB - J/247, 1836; DB - K/253, 1838; DB - L/282, 1840), Courthouse, Owingsville, Kentucky.
2. "Raccoon John Smith Once Owned Grubbs Home," *Lexington Herald,* 4 May 1969.
3. John Augustus Williams, *Life of Elder John Smith* (Cincinnati, R. W. Carroll and Co., 1870), 552.
4. Library of Everett Donaldson, Mt. Sterling, Kentucky, File of Isaac T. Reneau (copy of letter from John Smith to Isaac T. Reneau, dated July 5, 1852).
5. Ibid., File of Upper Spencer Church of Christ.
6. "A Letter From John Smith," *Discipliana,* Vol. 49, No. 3, (Fall 1989): 35-39. Note: original in Disciples of Christ Historical Society, Nashville, Tennessee, copy in files of Everett Donaldson, Mount Sterling, Kentucky.
7. Williams, 277.
8. M. C. Tiers, *The Portrait Gallery of Christian Preachers* (Cincinnati, By the Author, 1864), 72.
9. Oliver Taylor, *Historic Sullivan* (Johnson City, Tennessee: The Overmountain Press, 1909, reprint ed., 1988), xi, 175.
10. Tiers, 75-76.

BIBLIOGRAPHY

Allen, James Lane. *The Blue-Grass Region of Kentucky and Other Kentucky Articles*. Lexington, Kentucky: King Library Press, 1972.

Arrowood, Charles Flinn & Frederick Ely. *The Development of Modern Education*. New York: Prentice-Hall, Inc. 1946.

Becker, Mary Lamberton, ed. *Gulliver's Travels*, by Jonathan Swift (Cleveland/NY: The World Publishing Co., original, 1726, rep. ed., 1947.

Boles, H. Leo. *Biographical Sketches of Gospel Preachers*. Nashville: Gospel Advocate Company, 1932.

Bork, June Goldwin, *Wayne County Kentucky Pioneers— Biographical Sketches and Civil Court Records*. Monticello, Kentucky: by the author, 1974.

Bowles, John B. *The Great Revival*. Lexington, Kentucky: The University Press, 1972.

Boyd, Jr., Carl B., & Hazel Mason Boyd. *A History of Mt. Sterling, Kentucky, 1792-1918*. Mt. Sterling, Kentucky: by the authors, 1984.

Cartwright, Peter. *Autobiography of Peter Cartwright*. New York/Nashville: Abingdon Press, 1956.

Cherry, Thomas Crittenden. *Kentucky, The Pioneer State of the West*. Boston: D. C. Heath and Company, 1935.

Clark, Thomas D. *A History of Kentucky*. Lexington, Kentucky: The John Bradford Press, 1960.

Cochran, Louis. *The Frolic*. Lexington, Kentucky: The College of the Bible, 1964.

Conkwright, S. J. *Churches of Boone's Creek Baptist Association of Kentucky*. Winchester, Kentucky: By the Author, 1923.

Crismon, Leo Taylor. *Baptists in Kentucky, 1776-1976*. Middletown, Kentucky: Kentucky Baptist Convention, 1975.

Darnell, Ermina Jett. *Forks of Elkhorn Church*. Baltimore: Genealogical Publishing Company, Inc., 1980.

Davidson, James West & John E. Batchelor. 2 Vol. *A History of the Republic*. Englewood Falls, N. J. : Prentice-Hall, Inc., 1986.

DeMoss, Arthur S. *The Rebirth of America*. Arthur S. Demoss Foundation, 1986.

Donan, Philip P. *Life of Jacob Creath, Jr.* Indianapolis: reprinted., Religious Book Service.

Ferguson, Jack. *Early Times in Clinton County*. 2 Vol. Albany, Kentucky: by the author, 1986.

Garrison, Winfred Ernest. *Religion Follows the Frontier*. New York/ London: Harper & Brothers, 1931.

Garraty, John A. *The American Nation*. New York/London: Harper & Row, 1971.

Gaskins, Morris M. *A Lighthouse in the Wilderness*. Albany, Kentucky: The Clear Fork Baptist Church, 1972.

Hanna, William Herbert. *Thomas Campbell—Seceder and Christian Unity Advocate*. Joplin, Missouri: Rep. ed., College Press Publishing Company.

Hudson, Winthrop S. *Religion in America*. New York: Charles Scribner's Sons, 1978.

Kincaid, Robert L. *The Wilderness Road*. Middlesboro, Kentucky: Bobbs-Merrill Company, in "The American Trails" series, 1947.

Malone, Henry Thompson. *Cherokees of the Old South*. Athens: The University of Georgia Press.

Morison, Samuel Eliot. *The Oxford History of the American People*. New York: Oxford Press, 1965.

Masters, Frank. *A History of Baptists in Kentucky*. Louisville: Baptist Historical Society, 1953.

Mayer, Henry. *A Son of Thunder*. New York/Toronto: Franklin Watts, 1986.

Mead, Frank S. *Handbook of Denominations*. Nashville: Abingdon Press, 1951.

Mills, Dean. *Union on the King's Highway*. Joplin, Missouri: College Press Publishing Company, 1987.

Newman, A. H. *History of Baptist Churches in the United States*. Philadelphia: American Baptist Publication Society, 1898.

Nowlin, William Dudley. *Kentucky Baptist History—1770-1922*. Louisville: Baptist Book Concern, 1922.

Owens, Loulie Latimer. *Saints of Clay*. Columbia, S. C.: R. L. Bryan Company, 1971.

Perry, Samuel D. *South Fork Country*. Detroit: Harlo Press, 1983.

Randall, Max Ward. *The Great Awakenings and the Restoration Movement*. Joplin, Missouri: College Press Publishing Company, 1983.

Richardson, Robert. *Memoirs of Alexander Campbell*. 2 Vol. Philadelphia: J. B. Lippincott & Company, 1871.

Redford, A. H. *The History of Methodism in Kentucky*. 2 Vol. Nashville: Southern Methodist Publishing House, 1868.

Reid, Richard. *Historical Sketches of Montgomery County*. 1876; reprint ed., Lexington, Kentucky: The Woman's Club of Mt. Sterling, Kentucky, 1926.

Rogers, John. *The Biography of Elder Barton Warren Stone*. Cincinnati: J. A. and U. P. James, for the author, 1847.

Rogers, John. *The Biography of Elder J. T. Johnson*. Cincinnati: for the author, 1861.

Rogers, John. *The Life and Times of John Rogers, 1800-1867 of Carlisle, Kentucky*. Transcribed by Virginia Bell, Abridged by Roscoe M. Pierson and Richard L. Harrison, Jr. Lexington, Kentucky: Lexington Theological, 1984.

Rogers, John I. *Autobiography of Elder Samuel Rogers*. Cincinnati: Standard Publishing Company, 1880.

Rowe, F. L. ed. *Pioneer Sermons and Addresses*. Cincinnati: F. L. Rowe, 1908.

Sanders, Robert Stuart. *An Historical Sketch of Springfield Presbyterian Church*. Frankfort, Kentucky: Roberts Printing Company, 1954.

Semple, Robert Baylor. *History of the Baptists in Virginia*. Printed for the author, 1810; revised ed., Lafayette, Tennessee: Church History Research and Archives., 1976.

Shepherd, J. W. *The Church, The Falling Away, and The Restoration*. Nashville: Gospel Advocate Company, 1948.

Spencer, J. H. *A History of Kentucky Baptists*. 2 Vol. Printed for the Author, 1886; reprint ed., Lafayette, Tennessee.: Church History Research and Archives, 1976.

Summers, Lewis Preston. *History of Southwest Virginia*. Baltimore: Regional Publishing Company, 1971.

Taylor, Oliver. *Historic Sullivan*. Printed for the Author, 1909; reprint ed., Johnson City, Tennessee, Overmountain Press, 1988.

Tiers, M. C. *The Portrait Gallery of Christian Preachers*. Cincinnati, Ohio: By the Author, 1864.

Vaughn, Thomas M. *Memoirs of Rev. William Vaughn, D.D.* Louisville: Caperton and Gates, 1878.

Ver Steeg, Clarence L. & Hofstadter, Richard. *A People and A Nation*. New York/London: Harper & Row, 1977.

Walker, Garnett. *Exploring Wayne County*. Monticello, Kentucky: by the author, 1966.

Wallis, Charles L. ed. *Autobiography of Peter Cartwright*. New York/Nashville: Abingdon Press, 1956.

West, Earl Irvin. *The Search for the Ancient Order*. 4 Vol. Nashville, Tennessee: Gospel Advocate Company, 1949.

Williams, John Augustus. *Life of Elder John Smith*. Cincinnati, R.W. Carroll and Co., 1870; reprint ed., Indianapolis: Religious Book Service.

Wilson, Harold McKnight. *The Tinkling Spring*. Fisherville, Virginia: The Tinkling Spring and Heritage Presbyterian Churches, 1954.

Wood, Leonard, & others. *America: Its People and Values*. New York: Harcourt, Brace, Jovanovich, Inc., 1979.

PERIODICALS AND PAMPHLETS

An Address to the Different Religious Societies, on the Sacred Import of the Christian Name. (Lexington, Ky.: 1804; reprint, Lincoln, Ill.: Lincoln College Press (1969).

Christian History, Issue 23, Wheaton, Illinois.

Cumberland Gap, National Park Service, U. S. Department of the Interior.

Discipliana, Vol. 49, No. 3 (Fall 1989); Nashville, Tennessee: Disciples of Christ Historical Society.

Ford's Christian Repository, Vol. VI, No. 23 (1854).

Kentucky Historical Chronicle (1987).

Messenger, Vol. 136 (May 1987); Elgin, Ill: General Services Commission, Church of the Brethren General Board.

National Geographic Society, Vol. 172, No. 3, (September 1987).

Register of the Kentucky Historical Society, Vol. 79, No. 3, (Summer 1981).

The Apostolic Times, Vol. VIII, No 29 (July 1876).

The Christian Baptist, Vol. I, No. 1 (July 1823); Vol. V, No. 5 (May 1828); Vol. VI, No. 2 (Feb. 1829).

The Christian Messenger, Vol. VIII, No. 1 (Jan.1834).

The Disciple, St. Louis: Christian Board of Publications (Feb. 1988).

The Millennial Harbinger, Vol. I, No. 6 (June 1830); Vol. III, No. 3 (March 1832); Vol. IV, No. 9 (Sept. 1833); Vol. IV, No.10 (Oct. 1833); Vol. V, No. 9 (Sept. 1834); Vol. VI, No. 7 (July 1835); Vol. VI, No. 9 (Sept. 1835); Vol. VI, No. 11, (Nov. 1842); Vol. VII, No. 5 (May 1843); Vol. III, No. 6 (1846).

The Pennacle, National Park Service, U. S. Department of the Interior.

The World Evangelist, Florence, Alabama (Nov. 1987).

Bibliography

REFERENCE WORKS

Dictionary of Quotations and Proverbs. London: D. C. Browning, Compiler, 1951.
Encyclopedia of Southern Baptists. 2 Vol., Nashville: Broadman Press, 1958.
Kentucky County Maps. Lyndon Station, Wisconsin: C. J. Puetz.
The Bicentennial Almanac. Nashville/New York: Thomas Nelson, Inc., 1975.

NEWSPAPERS

Mt. Sterling Advocate, Mt. Sterling, Kentucky, 17 September 1975.
Sunday Herald-Leader, Lexington, Kentucky, 4 May 1969.

UNPUBLISHED MANUSCRIPTS AND OTHER RECORDS

Collection of Historical Materials—Library of Everett Donaldson, Mt. Sterling, Kentucky:
  "Brief History of Bethel Baptist Church"
  History of Antioch Christian Church
  Coons family file
  "Jacksboro Road," by Ruben Powell.
  Letters: Isaac T. Reneau; R. L. Roberts
  Minutes, Bethel Baptist Church, Wayne County, Kentucky. (1810-1817).
  Minutes, Elkhorn Baptist Association, (1826-1830).
  Minutes, North District Baptist Association, (1816-1828).
  New Bethlehem Christian Church Membership Roster, Historical Society, Mt. Sterling, Kentucky (1833-1870).
  "Old Fort Church"
  Survey Maps, Madison County, Alabama.
  "Taylor's History of Madison County, Alabama."
  Upper Spencer Church file
  Williams family file

Bibliography

LEGAL DOCUMENTS

Deed Book No. 16 & 17, Courthouse, Mt. Sterling, Kentucky.
Deed Book J/247, K/253, Courthouse, Owingsville, Kentucky.
Misc. deeds, Smith file, Library of Everett Donaldson, Mt. Sterling, Kentucky.
Misc. wills, deeds, Hon file, library of Everett Donaldson, Mt. Sterling, Kentucky.
Will Book D, Courthouse, Mt. Sterling, Kentucky.

INDEX

Antioch Church 163
Asbury, Francis 28
Barnes, Elijah 60
Barrier, Richard 55
Barrow, David 19, 77, 86, 101, 114
Bethel Baptist Church 56, 74, 75, 136
Bethlehem Church 163
Bledsoe, Moses 32, 77
Boone, Daniel 24, 83
Boone, Thomas 101, 116, 117
Botetourt County, Virginia 9, 22
Bracken Association 100
Bryan's Station Baptist Church 134
Burnett, David S. 120
Bush, Billy 32
Calhoun, John C. 62
Calvinism 11, 88
Campbell, Alexander 98, 101, 149
Campbell, Thomas 98, 120
Cane Ridge 93, 95, 96
Cane Ridge Revival 78
Cane Spring Baptist Church 100, 116
Cartwright, Peter 28
Chenault, David 89, 100, 106, 112
Church of Christ 94, 147
Clack, Spencer 122
Clark, George Rogers 25
Clay, Henry 62
Clear Fork Church 43, 72
Collins, Josiah 120
Concord Church 94
Coons, Jacob 103, 107
Coons, John 86, 107, 108

Coons, Matilda Jane Howe 104
Craig, Lewis 19, 31, 33, 34, 108
Creath, Jacob, Jr. 120, 130, 133, 141
Creath, Jacob, Sr. 70, 73, 132, 135, 167
Cumberland Gap 24, 25, 30
David's Fork 134
Davies, Samuel 13
Denton, Isaac 42, 56, 93, 159
Doublehead 36
East Union 146, 153
Edwards, Jonathan 13, 93
Elkhorn Baptist Assoc. 70, 73, 122, 139
Elkin, Robert 33, 34, 77
Ellis, Capt. William 32, 108
Fall, Philip S. 171
Ferrill, Robert 52, 72
Finley, John 25
Franklin Association 100
Franklin, Benjamin 21
Franklin, State of 21, 49
Frelinghuysen, Theodore J. 13
French, James 84, 106, 111, 116, 164
Fuller, Andrew 74, 90
Georgetown College 122
Goshen Baptist Church 114
Goshen Convention 118, 125
Grassy Lick Baptist Church 75, 82, 100
Great Awakening, First 12
Great Awakening, Second 92
Great Crossings 123, 140
Grosvenor, Benjamin 97
Haggard, Rice 96

Index

Hansford, Thomas 40, 71, 136
Harpe Gang 28, 40
Henry, Patrick 18, 20, 84
Hewitt, Josephus 120
Hickman, William 26
Hickory Flats, Alabama 63, 64, 66
Hill Street Church 145, 152, 154
Hon, Peter 139, 145, 149, 152
Horse Hollow 47, 48, 50, 58
Howe, Joseph Price 93, 103
Hurt, Nancy 74
Jacksboro Road 49
Jackson, Andrew 64
Jefferson, Thomas 18, 36
Johnson, John T. 123, 139, 151, 154
Johnson, Richard M. 62
Lee, Maria 169
Log Cabin College 13
Lulbegrud 83
Lulbegrud Baptist Church 75, 76, 83, 111, 116
Madison, James 18, 20
Marshall, Daniel 13
Mason, James 79, 115, 118, 125
McGready, James 92, 93
Miller Cemetery 66, 67
Miller, Anna 67
Montgomery, Gen. Richard 76
Mt. Sterling Baptist Church 76, 86, 114
New Lights 18, 94
Noel, Silas 122
North District Baptist Assoc. 77, 80, 88
O'Kelly, James 96

Old Lights 18
Panic of 1819 87
Parmley, Robert 49, 57
Parmleysville 48, 49, 50
Payne, Buckner 101, 120, 122
Payne, Jilson 83, 89
Payne, Thomas 14
Philadelphia Confession of Faith 55, 57, 77
Providence Church 32, 77
Raccoon Cognomen, The 170, 172
Ralls County, Missouri 135
Randolph, John 62
Regular Baptists 77, 93
Restoration Movement 22, 115
Ringo, Emma 169
Roberts, Dr. R.L. 148
Rogers, John 149, 152, 154, 156
Rogers, Samuel 29
Screven, William 13
Separatist Baptists 18, 77
Silas Church 122
Smith, George 9, 16, 21, 22, 35
Smith, Philip 56
Smith, Rebecca 10, 22
Somerset Church 122, 151
South Elkhorn Baptist Church 123
Spencer Creek Baptist Church 77, 86, 90
Springfield Church 93, 106
Springfield Presbytery, Last Will and Testament 95
Springfield Presbytery 95
Stepstone Creek 147, 148
Stockton's Valley 34
Stoddard, Solomon 12

Index

Stone, Barton W. 93, 154
Tates Creek Bapt. Assoc. 70
Taylor, John 25, 100
Tennent, William 13
Tories 14, 16
Townsend, Anne 53, 66
Traveling Churches 31, 33
Upper Spencer Church 8, 32
Vardeman, Jeremiah 39, 59, 69, 73, 100
Vaughn, William 102
Walker, Dr. Thomas 25, 26
Warder, Walter 100
Wayne, Gen. Anthony 76
Westminster Confession 94
White, Thomas 120
Whitefield, George 13, 18, 93
Whitley, Col. William 27, 39
Wilderness Road 24, 27
Williams, Col. John 88

EVERETT DONALDSON

Everett Donaldson was reared in rural Montgomery County, Kentucky, and spent his early years in the historic community of Upper Spencer.

He attended Freed-Hardeman University in Henderson, Tennessee, and earned undergraduate degrees from both Oklahoma Christian University in Oklahoma City, Oklahoma, and David Lipscomb University in Nashville, Tennessee. The Master of Arts degree was conferred upon him in 1956 by George Peabody College of Vanderbilt University, also located in Nashville. Additional graduate study at the University of Kentucky culminated in Rank I recognition as an educator in the state of Kentucky.

Donaldson began his thirty year career in education in a one room schoolhouse on the plains of Kansas. While teaching there he served as minister of the Kingman Church of Christ and directed Silver Maple Camp during the summer months.

In 1962 Donaldson returned to his native Montgomery County and continued in his profession as a high school history teacher. He became an administrator in 1966 and served as a principal on both the elementary and middle school levels.

Donaldson served as minister of the Queen Street Church of Christ in Mt. Sterling, Kentucky from 1962-68. He continued to preach at intervals when the congregation was without the services of a regular minister. For more than fourteen years he has served as one of the elders of the Queen Street Church.

Since his 1987 retirement from public school administration, Donaldson has served as a consultant for the Kentucky Department of Education and has engaged in extensive research on the life and work of Raccoon John Smith.

The father of four children, he is married to the former Temple Cope.